The PURSUIT of HOLINESS

JERRY BRIDGES

NAVPRESS

Discipleship Inside Out™

Discipleship Inside Out™

NavPress is the publishing ministry of The Navigators, an international Christian organization and leader in personal spiritual development. NavPress is committed to helping people grow spiritually and enjoy lives of meaning and hope through personal and group resources that are biblically rooted, culturally relevant, and highly practical.

**For a free catalog go to www.NavPress.com
or call 1.800.366.7788 in the United States or 1.800.839.4769 in Canada.**

Contents

Foreword   5

Preface   7

Before You Begin   9

SESSION ONE: Holiness Is for You   11
    Chapter One — Holiness Is for You
    Chapter Two — The Holiness of God

SESSION TWO: Holiness Is Not an Option   27
    Chapter Three — Holiness Is Not an Option

SESSION THREE: The Holiness of Christ   37
    Chapter Four — The Holiness of Christ

SESSION FOUR: The Battle for Holiness   45
    Chapter Five — A Change of Kingdoms
    Chapter Six — The Battle for Holiness

SESSION FIVE: God's Provision and Our Responsibility   61
    Chapter Seven — Help in the Daily Battle
    Chapter Eight — Obedience — Not Victory

SESSION SIX: Putting Sin to Death   75
    Chapter Nine — Putting Sin to Death

SESSION SEVEN: The Place of Personal Discipline   87
    Chapter Ten — The Place of Personal Discipline

SESSION EIGHT: Holiness in Body   97
    Chapter Eleven — Holiness in Body

Session Nine: Holiness in Spirit   105
    Chapter Twelve — Holiness in Spirit

Session Ten: Holiness and Our Wills   115
    Chapter Thirteen — Holiness and Our Wills
    Chapter Fourteen — Habits of Holiness

Session Eleven: Holiness and Faith   127
    Chapter Fifteen — Holiness and Faith

Session Twelve: Holiness in an Unholy World   137
    Chapter Sixteen — Holiness in an Unholy World
    Chapter Seventeen — The Joy of Holiness

A Further Word   149

Help for Group Leaders   151

Notes   159

About the Author   165

Foreword

Jerry Bridges has given the world one of the most incisive, appealing, and conscience-stirring treatises on scriptural holiness ever written. Without doubt, the Lord has enabled His servant to prepare a volume that will have a far-reaching impact upon the lives of countless numbers who read it.

The dominant theme of this heart-moving study is the need for increasing pursuit by believers for the holiness of life which God, whose holiness is ever gratefully remembered, can alone make possible. *Pursuit* is the key word which the author, whose personal pursuit has been long and strong, constantly repeats.

In the *Declaration of Independence*, Thomas Jefferson declared that one of the inherent and unalienable rights of men is "the pursuit of happiness." Professing Christians must be brought to realize that the preeminent desire and demand of God for us is that of the continual pursuit of holiness of life, and the reflection of His own holiness. "Be ye holy, for I am holy."

Well over 100 years ago, William Blake urged his readers to "put off holiness, and put on intellect." But divorced from divine holiness, intellect is like a ship without a captain, and doomed to disaster. In our quest for holiness the prayer must ever rise from the heart,

"Take my intellect and use
Every power as Thou shalt choose."

This is why we must warmly commend this compelling coverage of practical holiness, in which the author fully shows that the whole of life must be permeated with the holiness a thrice-holy God can impart.

Dr. Herbert Lockyer Sr.

Preface

A farmer plows his field, sows the seed, and fertilizes and cultivates — all the while knowing that in the final analysis he is utterly dependent on forces outside of himself. He knows he cannot cause the seed to germinate, nor can he produce the rain and sunshine for growing and harvesting the crop. For a successful harvest, he is dependent on these things from God.

Yet the farmer knows that unless he diligently pursues his responsibilities to plow, plant, fertilize, and cultivate, he cannot expect a harvest at the end of the season. In a sense he is in a partnership with God, and he will reap its benefits only when he has fulfilled his own responsibilities.

Farming is a joint venture between God and the farmer. The farmer cannot do what God must do, and God will not do what the farmer should do.

We can say just as accurately that the pursuit of holiness is a joint venture between God and the Christian. No one can attain any degree of holiness without God working in his life, but just as surely no one will attain it without effort on his own part. God has made it possible for us to walk in holiness. But He has given to us the responsibility of doing the walking; He does not do that for us.

We Christians greatly enjoy talking about the provision of God, how Christ defeated sin on the cross and gave us His Holy Spirit to empower us to victory over sin. But we do not as readily talk about our own responsibility to walk in holiness. Two primary reasons can be given for this.

First, we are simply reluctant to face up to our responsibility. We prefer to leave that to God. We pray for victory when we know we should be acting in obedience.

The second reason is that we do not understand the proper distinction between God's provision and our own responsibility for holiness. I struggled for a number of years with the question, "What am I to do myself, and what am I to rely on God to do?" Only as I came to see what the Bible teaches on this question, and then faced up to my own responsibility, did I see any progress in the "pursuit of holiness."

The title for this book comes from the biblical command, "Pursue holiness, for without holiness no one will see the Lord" (Hebrews 12:14, author's paraphrase). The word *pursue* suggests two thoughts: first, that diligence and effort are required; and second, that it is a lifelong task. These two thoughts form a dual theme throughout this book. While seeking to set forth clearly and accurately God's provision for our holiness, I have deliberately stressed our responsibility, feeling that this is an emphasis sorely needed among Christians today. At the same time I have sought to emphasize that holiness is a process, something we never completely attain in this life. Rather, as we begin to conform to the will of God in one area of life, He reveals to us our need in another area. That is why we will always be pursuing — as opposed to attaining — holiness in this life.

In addition to my own personal Bible study on the subject of holiness, I have profited greatly from the writings of the Puritans — and those who followed in their school of thought — on the subject of holiness. On numerous occasions I have quoted directly from them and have so indicated in the appropriate footnotes. In other instances their phraseology has crept into my own manner of expression. This is particularly true of the writings of John Owen and of Dr. D. Martyn Lloyd-Jones of London, both of whose writings on this subject have been of invaluable personal blessing.

I do not profess to know all about this subject, nor can I claim all that much personal progress. Many times while writing this book I have had to first make application to my own life. But what I have discovered has been of invaluable help to me in my own pursuit of holiness, and I trust will be of help to all who read it.

To explore more fully the scriptural principles of holiness, which I studied in writing this book, "I encourage the reader to work through the accompanying study guide."

Finally, I want to express my thanks to Mrs. Peggy Sharp and Miss Linda Dicks, who patiently typed and retyped the various drafts of the manuscript.

Before You Begin

What is holiness? Do we fully understand our responsibility to live a holy life? Why do we experience defeat in the struggle against sin? What has God provided to help us overcome sin?

To help answer these questions, the Bible-study sessions for *The Pursuit of Holiness* lead you toward personal discovery of God's principles for holy living. Each session will engage you in direct study of many Scripture passages on which the book is based.

The most profitable way of doing this study is to complete the study questions before you meet with your group. (If you lead the group, the section at the back of the book called "Help for Group Leaders" gives practical suggestions for guiding others through this study.)

This study consists of twelve sessions, which encompass all seventeen chapters in *The Pursuit of Holiness*. For each, you will read a chapter or chapters from the book, look up Scripture passages, and answer questions about the session's topic. Then you will plan a way to apply the truths of the session to your life. Within each session is an optional question for further study of the Scriptures.

Before beginning each session, ask God to clarify the Scriptures to you and to reveal Himself to you in new ways.

Use a pen or pencil to underline or mark key statements as you read the book. This practice can be one of the most profitable for you in each session, allowing you to expand upon the material presented in the text. During your reading, jot down any

- Observations about the text that you want to remember
- Additional Scripture passages or incidents from your life or the lives of others that illustrate the truths of the session
- Questions that come to your mind

As you answer the questions for each session and prepare to write an application at the end, ask yourself these questions:

- What do these passages teach about God's will for a holy life?
- How does my life reflect the truths I see in Scripture?
- What definite steps of action do I need to take to obey God?
- How would God want me to rely on His help to take these steps?

Write down not only the scriptural truth you want to apply, but also a practical specific statement and plan for making the application.

As you learn more about our calling from "the high and exalted One, who lives forever, whose name is Holy" (Isaiah 57:15, NASB), may you experience new commitment and joy in holy living.

Holiness Is for You

Read the following portion of *The Pursuit of Holiness*. In the margins, record observations, illustrations, or questions that come to mind as you read. Then answer the study questions that follow the reading.

Chapter One: Holiness Is for You

*For sin shall not be your master, because you
are not under law, but under grace.*
ROMANS 6:14

Notes and Observations

The shrill ring of the telephone shattered the stillness of the beautiful, crisp Colorado morning. On the other end was one of those utterly impossible individuals God seems to have sprinkled around here on earth to test the grace and patience of His children.

He was in top form that morning—arrogant, impatient, demanding. I hung up the phone seething inside with anger, resentment, and perhaps even hatred. Grabbing my jacket, I walked out into the cold air to try to regain my composure. The quietness of my soul, so carefully cultivated in my "quiet time" with God that morning, had been ripped into shreds and replaced with a volatile, steaming emotional volcano.

As my emotions subsided, my anger turned to utter discouragement. It was only 8:30 in the morning and my day was ruined. Not only was I discouraged, I was confused. Only two hours before, I had read Paul's emphatic declaration, "For sin shall not be your master, because you are not under law, but under grace." But despite this nice-sounding promise of victory over sin, there I was locked in the vise-like grip of anger and resentment.

"Does the Bible really have any answers for real life?" I asked

myself that morning. With all my heart I desired to live an obedient, holy life; yet there I was utterly defeated by one phone call.

Perhaps this incident has a familiar ring to you. The circumstances probably differed, but your reaction was similar. Perhaps
your problem was anger with your children, or a temper at work,
or an immoral habit you can't overcome, or maybe several "besetting sins" that dog you day in and day out.

Whatever your particular sin problem (or problems), the
Bible does have the answer for you. There is hope. You and I
can walk in obedience to God's Word and live a life of holiness.
In fact, as we will see in the next chapter, God expects every
Christian to live a holy life. But holiness is not only expected; it
is the promised birthright of every Christian. Paul's statement
is true. Sin shall not be our master.

The concept of holiness may seem a bit archaic to our cur-
rent generation. To some minds the very word *holiness* brings
images of bunned hair, long skirts, and black stockings. To
others the idea is associated with a repugnant "holier than
thou" attitude. Yet holiness is very much a scriptural idea. The
word *holy* in various forms occurs more than 600 times in the
Bible. One entire book, Leviticus, is devoted to the subject, and
the idea of holiness is woven elsewhere throughout the fabric of
Scripture. More important, God specifically commands us to
be holy (see Leviticus 11:44).

The idea of exactly how to be holy has suffered from many
false concepts. In some circles, holiness is equated with a series
of specific prohibitions—usually in such areas as smoking, drinking, and dancing. The list of prohibitions varies depending on
the group. When we follow this approach to holiness, we are in
danger of becoming like the Pharisees with their endless lists
of trivial do's and don'ts, and their self-righteous attitude. For
others, holiness means a particular style of dress and mannerisms.
And for still others, it means unattainable perfection, an idea that
fosters either delusion or discouragement about one's sin.

All of these ideas, while accurate to some degree, miss the

true concept. To be holy is to be morally blameless.[1] It is to be separated from sin and, therefore, consecrated to God. The word signifies "separation to God, and the conduct befitting those so separated."[2]

Perhaps the best way of understanding the concept of holiness is to note how writers of the New Testament used the word. In 1 Thessalonians 4:3-7, Paul used the term in contrast to a life of immorality and impurity. Peter used it in contrast to living according to the evil desires we had when we lived outside of Christ (1 Peter 1:14-16). John contrasted one who is holy with those who do wrong and are vile (Revelation 22:11). To live a holy life, then, is to live a life in conformity to the moral precepts of the Bible and in contrast to the sinful ways of the world. It is to live a life characterized by the "[putting] off of your old self, which is being corrupted by its deceitful desires . . . and [putting] on the new self, created to be like God in true righteousness and holiness" (Ephesians 4:22,24).

If holiness, then, is so basic to the Christian life, why do we not experience it more in daily living? Why do so many Christians feel constantly defeated in their struggle with sin? Why does the Church of Jesus Christ so often seem to be more conformed to the world around it than to God?

At the risk of oversimplification, the answers to these questions can be grouped into three basic problem areas.

Our first problem is that *our attitude toward sin is more self-centered than God-centered.* We are more concerned about our own "victory" over sin than we are about the fact that our sins grieve the heart of God. We cannot tolerate failure in our struggle with sin chiefly because we are success-oriented, not because we know it is offensive to God.

W. S. Plumer said, "We never see sin aright until we see it as against God. . . . All sin is against God in this sense: that it is His law that is broken, His authority that is despised, His government that is set at naught. . . . Pharaoh and Balaam, Saul and Judas each said, 'I have sinned'; but the returning prodigal said, 'I have sinned *against heaven* and before thee'; and David said, 'Against Thee, Thee only have I sinned.'"[3]

God wants us to walk in *obedience*—not victory. Obedience is oriented toward God; victory is oriented toward self. This may seem to be merely splitting hairs over semantics, but there is a subtle, self-centered attitude at the root of many of our difficulties with sin. Until we face this attitude and deal with it, we will not consistently walk in holiness.

This is not to say God doesn't want us to experience victory, but rather to emphasize that victory is a byproduct of obedience. As we concentrate on living an obedient, holy life, we will certainly experience the joy of victory over sin.

Our second problem is that *we have misunderstood "living by faith"* (Galatians 2:20) to mean that no effort at holiness is required on our part. In fact, sometimes we have even suggested that any effort on our part is "of the flesh."

The words of J. C. Ryle, Bishop of Liverpool from 1880 to 1900, are instructive to us on this point: "Is it wise to proclaim in so bald, naked, and unqualified a way as many do, that the holiness of converted people is by faith only, and not at all by personal exertion? Is it according to the proportion of God's Word? I doubt it. That faith in Christ is the root of all holiness . . . no well-instructed Christian will ever think of denying. But surely the Scriptures teach us that in following holiness the true Christian needs personal exertion and work as well as faith."[4]

We must face the fact that we have a personal responsibility for our walk of holiness. One Sunday our pastor in his sermon said words to this effect: "You can put away that habit that has mastered you if you truly desire to do so." Because he was referring to a particular habit which was no problem to me, I quickly agreed with him in my mind. But then the Holy Spirit said to me, "And you can put away the sinful habits that plague you if you will accept your personal responsibility for them." Acknowledging that I did have this responsibility turned out to be a milestone for me in my own pursuit of holiness.

Our third problem is that *we do not take some sin seriously*. We have mentally categorized sins into that which is unacceptable and that which may be tolerated a bit. An incident that occurred just as this book was nearing completion illustrates this problem. Our office was using a mobile home as temporary office space, pending the delayed completion of new facilities. Because our property is not zoned for mobile homes, we were required to obtain a variance permit to occupy the trailer. The permit had to be renewed several times. The last permit renewal expired just as the new facilities were completed, but before we had time to move out in an orderly manner. This precipitated a crisis for the department occupying the trailer.

At a meeting where this problem was discussed, the question was asked, "What difference would it make if we didn't move that department for a few days?" Well, what difference would it make? After all, the trailer was tucked in behind some hills where no one would see it. And legally we didn't have to move the trailer; just vacate it. So what difference would it make if we overstayed our permit a few days? Isn't insistence on obeying the letter of the law nit-picking legalism?

But the Scripture says it is "the little foxes that ruin the vineyards" (Song of Songs 2:15). It is compromise on the little issues that leads to greater downfalls. And who is to say that a little ignoring of civil law is not a serious sin in the sight of God?

In commenting on some of the more minute Old Testament dietary laws God gave to the children of Israel, Andrew Bonar said,

> It is not the importance of the thing, but the majesty of the Lawgiver, that is to be the standard of obedience. . . . Some, indeed, might reckon such minute and arbitrary rules as these as trifling. But the principle involved in obedience or disobedience was none other than the same principle which was tried in Eden at the foot of the forbidden tree. It is really this: Is the Lord

15

to be obeyed in *all* things whatsoever He commands? Is He a holy Lawgiver? Are His creatures bound to give implicit assent to His will?[5]

Are we willing to call sin "sin" not because it is big or little, but because God's law forbids it? We cannot categorize sin if we are to live a life of holiness. God will not let us get away with that kind of attitude.

These three problems will be addressed in greater detail in subsequent sessions of this book. But before moving on, take time to settle these issues in your heart, right now. Will you begin to look at sin as an offense against a holy God, instead of as a personal defeat only? Will you begin to take personal responsibility for your sin, realizing that as you do, you must depend on the grace of God? And will you decide to obey God in all areas of life, however insignificant the issue may be?

As we move on, we will first consider the holiness of God. This is where holiness begins—not with ourselves, but with God. It is only as we see His holiness, His absolute purity and moral hatred of sin, that we will be gripped by the awfulness of sin against the Holy God. To be gripped by that fact is the first step in our pursuit of holiness.

Chapter Two: The Holiness of God

But just as he who called you is holy, so be holy in all you do; for it is written: "Be holy, because I am holy."
I Peter 1:15-16

God has called every Christian to a holy life. There are no exceptions to this call. It is not a call only to pastors, missionaries, and a few dedicated Sunday school teachers. Every Christian of every nation, whether rich or poor, learned or unlearned, influential or totally unknown, is called to be holy.

The Christian plumber and the Christian banker, the unsung homemaker and the powerful head of state are all alike called to be holy.

This call to a holy life is based on the fact that God Himself is holy. Because God is holy, He requires that we be holy. Many Christians have what we might call a "cultural holiness." They adapt to the character and behavior pattern of Christians around them. As the Christian culture around them is more or less holy, so these Christians are more or less holy. But God has not called us to be like those around us. He has called us to be like Himself. Holiness is nothing less than conformity to the character of God.[6]

As used in Scripture, holiness describes both the majesty of God and the purity and moral perfection of His nature. Holiness is one of His attributes;[7] that is, holiness is an essential part of the nature of God. His holiness is as necessary as His existence, or as necessary, for example, as His wisdom or omniscience. Just as He cannot but *know* what is right, so He cannot but *do* what is right.

We ourselves do not always know what is right, what is just and fair. At times we agonize over decisions having moral overtones. "What is the right thing to do?" we ask. God, of course, never faces this predicament. His perfect knowledge precludes any uncertainty on what is right and wrong.

But sometimes, even when we know what is right, there is a reluctance on our part to do it. The right action may involve sacrifice, or a blow to our pride (for example, when we know we should confess a sin to someone), or some other obstacle. But here again, this is never true with God. God never vacillates. He always does what is just and right without the slightest hesitation. It is impossible in the very nature of God for Him to do otherwise.

God's holiness then is perfect freedom from all evil. We say a garment is clean when it is free from any spot, or gold is pure when all dross has been refined from it. In this manner we can

17

think of the holiness of God as the absolute absence of any evil in Him. John said, "God is light; in him there is no darkness at all" (1 John 1:5). Light and darkness, when used this way in Scripture, have moral significance. John is telling us that God is absolutely free from any moral evil and that He is Himself the essence of moral purity.

The holiness of God also includes His perfect conformity to His own divine character. That is, all of His thoughts and actions are consistent with His holy character. By contrast, consider our own lives. Over time, as we mature in the Christian life, we develop a certain degree of Christian character. We grow in such areas as truthfulness, purity, and humility. But we do not always act consistently with our character. We tell a lie or allow ourselves to get trapped into a series of impure thoughts. Then we are dismayed with ourselves for these actions because they are inconsistent with our character. This never happens to God. He always acts consistently with His holy character. And it is this standard of holiness that God has called us to when He says, "Be holy, because I am holy."

The absolute holiness of God should be of great comfort and assurance to us. If God is perfectly holy, then we can be confident that His actions toward us are always perfect and just. We are often tempted to question God's actions and complain that He is unfair in His treatment of us. This is the devil's lie, the same thing he did to Eve. He essentially told her, "God is being unfair to you" (Genesis 3:4-5). But it is impossible in the very nature of God that He should ever be unfair. Because He is holy, all His actions are holy.

We must accept by faith the fact that God is holy, even when trying circumstances make it appear otherwise. To complain against God is in effect to deny His holiness and to say He is not fair. In the seventeenth century Stephen Charnock said, "It is less injury to Him to deny His being, than to deny the purity of it; the one makes Him no God, the other a deformed, unlovely, and a detestable God . . . he that saith

God is not holy speaks much worse than he that saith there is no God at all."[8]

I still vividly recall how God first dealt with me over twenty-five years ago about complaining against Him. In response to His will, I had settled in San Diego, California, and had begun to look for a job. When several weeks went by without success, I mentally began to accuse God. "After all, I gave up my plans in order to do His will and now He has let me down." God graciously directed my attention to Job 34:18-19: "Is he not the One who says to kings, 'You are worthless,' and to nobles, 'You are wicked,' who shows no partiality to princes and does not favor the rich over the poor, for they are all the work of his hands?" As soon as I read that passage I immediately fell to my knees confessing to Him my terrible sin of complaining and questioning His holiness. God mercifully forgave and the next day I received two job offers.

Acknowledging His holiness is one of the ways we are to praise God. According to John's vision of heaven described in Revelation 4, the four living creatures around God's throne never stop saying, "Holy, holy, holy is the Lord God Almighty, who was, and is, and is to come" (Revelation 4:8). The seraphim in Isaiah's vision of God's glory also uttered this threefold ascription of God's holiness (Isaiah 6:3). When Moses was praising God for the deliverance of the Israelites from Pharaoh's army, he also sang of God's holiness:

> Who among the gods is like you, O LORD?
>   Who is like you—
>   majestic in holiness,
>   awesome in glory,
>   working wonders? (Exodus 15:11)

God is often called in Scripture by such names as the Holy One, or the Holy One of Israel.[9] Holy, according to Stephen Charnock,[10] is used more often as a prefix to His name than any other attribute. Holiness is God's crown. Imagine for a moment that God possessed omnipotence (infinite power), omniscience (perfect and complete knowledge), and omnipresence (everywhere present), but without perfect holiness. Such a one could no longer be described as God. Holiness is the perfection of all His other attributes: His power is holy power; His mercy is holy mercy; His wisdom is holy wisdom. It is His holiness more than any other attribute that makes Him worthy of our praise.

But God demands more than that we acknowledge His holiness. He says to us, "Be holy, because I am holy." God rightfully demands perfect holiness in all of His moral creatures. It cannot be otherwise. He cannot possibly ignore or approve of any evil committed. He cannot for one moment relax His perfect standard of holiness. Rather He must say, as He does say, "So be holy in *all* you do" (1 Peter 1:15, emphasis added). The prophet Habakkuk declared, "Your eyes are too pure to look on evil; you cannot tolerate wrong" (Habakkuk 1:13). Because God is holy, He can never excuse or overlook any sin we commit, however small it may be.

Sometimes we try to justify to God some action which our own conscience calls into question. But if we truly grasp the significance of God's perfect holiness, both in Himself and in His demands of us, we will readily see we can never justify before Him even the slightest deviation from His perfect will. God does not accept the excuse, "Well, that's just the way I am," or even the more hopeful statement, "Well, I'm still growing in that area of my life."

No, God's holiness does not make allowance for minor flaws or shortcomings in our personal character. Well might we Christians, though justified solely through the righteousness of Christ, ponder carefully the words of the writer to the Hebrews: "Make every effort . . . to be holy; without holiness no one will see the Lord" (Hebrews 12:14).

Because God is holy, He cannot ever tempt us to sin. "When

tempted, no one should say, 'God is tempting me.' For God cannot be tempted by evil, nor does he tempt anyone" (James 1:13). Probably none of us ever imagines that God is actively soliciting us to do evil, but we may feel that God has put us in a situation where we have no choice.

King Saul felt this way in his first major campaign against the Philistines (1 Samuel 13). Before going into battle Saul was to wait seven days for the prophet Samuel to come and offer a burnt offering and ask the favor of the Lord. Saul waited the seven days for Samuel. When he didn't come, Saul became anxious and took it on himself to offer the burnt offering. Saul felt he had no alternative. The people were fearful and had begun to scatter; the Philistines were assembling for battle; Samuel was overdue. Something had to be done! God had put him in a place where he had no choice, it seemed, but to disobey God's explicit instructions.

But because Saul disobeyed God's express will, he lost his kingdom (1 Samuel 13:13-14). What about us? Do we sometimes feel we have no choice but to shade the truth a little, or commit just a slightly dishonest act? When we feel this way, we are in effect saying that God is tempting us to sin, that He has put us in a position where we have no alternative.

People under authority are particularly vulnerable to this temptation. Supervisors often put pressure on those below them to commit dishonest or unethical acts. As a young officer in the Navy, I faced this temptation. For a few pounds of coffee to the right people, our ship could get "free" all kinds of valuable equipment we needed to do our job. "And after all," so the reasoning went, "it all belongs to the Navy." I finally had to stand up to my commanding officer and, in jeopardy to my Navy career, tell him I could have no part of that.

Because God is holy, He hates sin. Hate is such a strong word we dislike using it. We reprove our children for saying they hate someone. Yet when it comes to God's attitude toward sin, only a strong word such as hate conveys an adequate depth of meaning. Speaking of various sins in Israel, God says, "For all these things are what I hate" (Zechariah 8:17, NASB). Hatred is a legitimate emotion when it comes to sin. In fact, the more we ourselves grow in holiness, the more we hate sin. David said, "I gain understanding from your precepts; therefore I hate every wrong path" (Psalm 119:104). Now if that is true of a man, think of God. As we grow in holiness, we grow in hatred of sin; and God, being infinitely holy, has an infinite hatred of sin.

We often say, "God hates the sin but loves the sinner." This is blessedly true, but too often we quickly rush over the first half of this statement to get to the second. We cannot escape the fact that God hates our sins. We may trifle with our sins or excuse them, but God hates them.

Therefore every time we sin, we are doing something God hates. He hates our lustful thoughts, our pride and jealousy, our outbursts of temper, and our rationalization that the end justifies the means. We need to be gripped by the fact that God hates all these things. We become so accustomed to our sins we sometimes lapse into a state of peaceful coexistence with them, but God never ceases to hate them.

We need to cultivate in our own hearts the same hatred of sin God has. Hatred of sin as sin, not just as something disquieting or defeating to ourselves, but as displeasing to God, lies at the root of all true holiness. We must cultivate the attitude of Joseph, who said when he was tempted, "How then could I do such a wicked thing and sin against God?" (Genesis 39:9).

God hates sin wherever He finds it, in saint and sinner alike. He does not hate sin in one person and overlook it in another. He judges each man's works impartially (1 Peter 1:17). In fact, biblical evidence indicates that God may judge the sins of His saints more severely than those of the world. David was a man after God's own heart (Acts 13:22), yet after his sin against Uriah, he was told, "Now therefore, the sword will never depart from your house" (2 Samuel 12:10). Moses, for one act of unbelief, was excluded from the land of Canaan despite many years of faithful service. Jonah, for his disobedience, was cast into a horrible prison in the stomach of a giant fish for three days and nights, that he might learn not to run from the command of God.

In the deceitfulness of our hearts, we sometimes play with temptation by entertaining the thought that we can always confess and later ask forgiveness. Such thinking is exceedingly dangerous. God's judgment is without partiality. He never overlooks our sin. He never decides not to bother since the sin is only a small one. No, God hates sin intensely whenever and wherever He finds it.

Frequent contemplation on the holiness of God and His consequent hatred of sin is a strong deterrent against trifling with sin. We are told to live our lives on earth as strangers in reverence and fear (I Peter 1:17). Granted, the love of God to us through Jesus Christ should be our primary motivation to holiness. But a motivation prompted by God's hatred of sin and His consequent judgment on it is no less biblical.

The holiness of God is an exceedingly high standard, a perfect standard. But it is nevertheless one that He holds us to. He cannot do less. While it is true that He accepts us solely through the merit of Christ, God's standard for our character, attitudes, affections, and actions is, "Be holy, because I am holy." We must take this seriously if we are to grow in holiness.

Holiness Is for You

(Chapters 1 and 2)

STUDY QUESTIONS

1. Look again at the three reasons why we do not experience more personal holiness (pages 13-15). Which of them applies most to your life? Can you think of other reasons?

2. Look up the following verses and meditate on what each one says about God's holiness. Copy from your Bible the verse or verses which are the most meaningful to you, and explain why they are.

    •   Exodus 15:11; Leviticus 19:1-2; Psalm 89:35; Isaiah 57:15; 1 Peter 1:14-16

3. Write a sentence for each of the following verses telling what it teaches about God's holiness.

    •   Habakkuk 1:13

    •   Zechariah 8:17

    •   James 1:13

4. (*For additional study*) Look up the following verses, analyzing what each one teaches about God's holiness or holiness in the Christian. Copy from your Bible the passages which are most helpful to you, and explain why they are.

    •   1 Samuel 13:13-14; Psalm 51:4; Isaiah 6:1-5; 40:25; Jeremiah 51:5; Ezekiel 39:7; Romans 6:14; 1 John 1:5; Revelation 4:8; 22:11

5. In your own words write a definition of holiness.

6.   What application of the truths of this session do you want to make in your life?

Holiness Is Not an Option

Read the following portion of *The Pursuit of Holiness*. In the margins, record observations, illustrations, or questions that come to mind as you read. Then answer the study questions that follow the reading.

Chapter 3: Holiness Is Not an Option

Make every effort to live in peace with all men and to be holy;
without holiness no one will see the Lord.
Hebrews 12:14

Notes and Observations

J ust what do these words, "without holiness no one will see the Lord" actually mean? Does our salvation in the final analysis depend to some degree on our attaining some level of personal holiness?

On this question the Scripture is clear on two points. First, the best Christians can never in themselves merit salvation through their personal holiness. Our righteous deeds are like filthy garments in the light of God's holy law (Isaiah 64:6). Our best works are stained and polluted with imperfection and sin. As one of the saints of several centuries ago put it, "Even our tears of repentance need to be washed in the blood of the lamb."

Second, Scripture repeatedly refers to the obedience and righteousness of Christ on our behalf. "For just as through the disobedience of the one man the many were made sinners, so also through the obedience of the one man the many will be made righteous" (Romans 5:19). "For Christ died for sins once for all, the righteous for the unrighteous, to bring you to God" (1 Peter 3:18). These two passages teach a twofold aspect of Christ's work on our behalf. They are often referred to as His active and His passive obedience.

27

Active obedience means Christ's sinless life here on earth, His perfect obedience and absolute holiness. This perfect life is credited to those who trust in Him for their salvation. His passive obedience refers to His death on the cross through which He fully paid the penalty for our sins and placated the wrath of God toward us. In Hebrews 10:5-9 we read that Christ came to do the will of the Father. Then the writer said, "And by that will, *we have been made holy* through the sacrifice of the body of Jesus Christ once for all" (Hebrews 10:10, emphasis added). So we see that our holiness before God depends entirely on the work of Jesus Christ for us, by God's will.

Does Hebrews 12:14 refer then to this holiness which we have in Christ? No, for at this point the writer speaks of a holiness which we are to strive after; we are to "make every effort . . . to be holy." And without this holiness, the writer says, no one will see the Lord.

Scripture speaks of both a holiness which we have in Christ before God, and a holiness which we are to strive after. These two aspects of holiness complement one another, for our salvation is a salvation to holiness: "For God did not call us to be impure, but to live a holy life" (1 Thessalonians 4:7). To the Corinthians Paul wrote: "To the church of God in Corinth, to those sanctified in Christ Jesus and called *to be holy*" (1 Corinthians 1:2, emphasis added). The word *sanctified* here means "made holy." That is, we are through Christ *made* holy in our standing before God, and *called* to be holy in our daily lives.

So the writer of Hebrews is telling us to take seriously the necessity of personal, practical holiness. When the Holy Spirit comes into our lives at our salvation, He comes to make us holy in practice. If there is not, then, at least a yearning in our hearts to live a holy life pleasing to God, we need to seriously question whether our faith in Christ is genuine.

It is true that this desire for holiness may be only a spark at the beginning. But that spark should grow till it becomes a flame—a desire to live a life wholly pleasing to God. True salvation brings with it a desire to be made holy. When God saves us through Christ, He not only saves us from the penalty of sin, but also from its dominion. Bishop Ryle said, "I doubt, indeed, whether we have any warrant for saying that a man can possibly be converted without being consecrated to God. More consecrated he doubtless can be, and will be as his grace increases; but if he was not consecrated to God in the very day that he was converted and born again, I do not know what conversion means."[1]

The whole purpose of our salvation is that we be "holy and blameless in his sight" (Ephesians 1:4). To continue to live in sin as a Christian is to go contrary to God's very purpose for our salvation. One of the writers of three centuries ago put it like this: "What a strange kind of salvation do they desire that care not for holiness. . . . They would be saved by Christ and yet be out of Christ in a fleshly state. . . . They would have their sins forgiven, not that they may walk with God in love, in time to come, but that they may practice their enmity against Him without any fear of punishment."[2]

Holiness, then, is not necessary as a *condition* of salvation—that would be salvation by works—but as a *part* of salvation that is received by faith in Christ. The angel said to Joseph, "You are to give him the name Jesus [which means 'Jehovah is salvation'], because he will save his people from their sins" (Matthew 1:21).

Therefore, we may say that no one can trust in Jesus Christ for true salvation unless he trusts in Him for holiness. This does not mean the desire for holiness must be a conscious desire at the time a person comes to Christ, but rather it means that the Holy Spirit who creates within us saving faith also creates within us the desire for holiness. He simply does not create one without the other.

Paul said, "For the grace of God that brings salvation has appeared to all men. It teaches us to say 'No' to ungodliness and worldly passions, and to live self-controlled, upright and godly lives in this present age" (Titus 2:11-12). The same grace that brings salvation teaches us to renounce ungodly living. We cannot receive half of God's grace. If we have experienced it at all, we will experience not only forgiveness of our sins but also freedom from sin's dominion.

This is the point James is making in his hard-to-understand passage on faith and works (James 2:14-26). He is simply telling us that a "faith" that does not result in works—in a holy life, in other words—is not a living faith but a dead one, no better than that which the demons possess.

God's nature demands holiness in the life of a Christian. When He calls us to salvation, He calls us to fellowship with Himself and His Son Jesus Christ (1 John 1:3). But God is light; in Him is no darkness at all (1 John 1:5). How then can we have fellowship with Him if we continue to walk in darkness?

Holiness then is required for *fellowship with God*. David asked the question, "LORD, who may dwell in your sanctuary? Who may live on your holy hill?" (Psalm 15:1). That is to say, "Lord, who may live in fellowship with You?" The answer given in the next four verses may be summarized as "he who leads a holy life."

Prayer is a vital part of our fellowship with God; yet the psalmist said, "If I had cherished sin in my heart, the Lord would not have listened" (Psalm 66:18). To regard wickedness is to cherish some sin, to love it to the extent that I am not willing to part with it. I know it is there, yet I justify it in some way like the child who says, "Well, he hit me first." When we are holding on to some sin, we are not pursuing holiness and we cannot have fellowship with God.

God does not require a perfect, sinless life to have fellowship with Him, but He does require that we be serious about holiness, that we grieve over sin in our lives instead of justifying it, and that we earnestly pursue holiness as a way of life.

Holiness is also required for *our own well-being*. Scripture says, "The Lord disciplines those he loves, and he punishes everyone he accepts as a son" (Hebrews 12:6). This statement presupposes our need of discipline, for God is not capricious in administering it. He disciplines us because we need discipline.

To persist in disobedience is to increase our necessity for discipline. Some of the Corinthian Christians persisted in disobedience to the point where God had to take their lives (1 Corinthians 11:30).

David described the discipline of the Lord this way: "When I kept silent, my bones wasted away through my groaning all day long. For day and night your hand was heavy upon me; my strength was sapped as in the heat of summer" (Psalm 32:3-4).

When God speaks to us about some sin, we need to heed and take action. To fail to deal with that sin is to risk incurring His hand of discipline. One icy morning as I was turning into the driveway of The Navigators headquarters where I work, my car skidded out of control into a corner fence post. Someone else in a similar predicament had already bent the post, and I only increased the angle. I said nothing to the property manager, despite several gentle proddings from God. Two weeks later I had another slight accident. After over fifteen years of accident-free driving, I knew God was trying to get my attention, so I called up the property manager, reported my first accident, and offered to pay for a new fence post. As Peter said, "Live your lives as strangers here in reverent fear" (1 Peter 1:17). God is serious about holiness in the lives of His people, and He will discipline us to attain it.

Holiness is also necessary for *effective service to God*. Paul wrote to Timothy, "If a man cleanses himself from [ignoble purposes], he will be an instrument for noble purposes, made holy, useful to the Master and prepared to do any good work" (2 Timothy 2:21). Holiness and usefulness are linked together. We cannot bring our service to God in an unclean vessel.

The One who makes our service effective and who empowers us for service is the Holy Spirit. Note well that He is called the *Holy* Spirit, or the Spirit of Holiness. When we indulge our sinful natures and dwell in unholiness, the Spirit of God is grieved (Ephesians 4:30) and will not prosper our service. These are not times when we fall into temptation and imme-

31

diately seek God's forgiveness and cleansing, but lives that are characterized by unholy living.

Holiness also is necessary for our *assurance of salvation*—not at the moment of salvation, but over the course of our lives. True faith will always show itself by its fruits. "Therefore, if anyone is in Christ, he is a new creation" (2 Corinthians 5:17).

I recall a young man, a fairly new Christian, whose father was visiting him. He had not seen his father for several years and not since he had become a Christian. He was eager to share his newfound faith with his dad, and we prayed together that he might be an effective witness to his father.

Several days later I asked him how it had gone with his witness. He told me his dad had claimed to have trusted Christ as his Savior when he "went forward" at age ten in an evangelistic meeting. I asked the young man, "In all the years you were growing up, did you ever see any evidence that your father was a Christian?" His answer was "No." What reason have we to put confidence in that man's salvation? He was almost sixty and had never once given his son any evidence that he was a Christian.

The only safe evidence that we are in Christ is a holy life. John said everyone who has within him the hope of eternal life purifies himself just as Christ is pure (1 John 3:3). Paul said, "Those who are led by the Spirit of God are sons of God" (Romans 8:14). If we know nothing of holiness, we may flatter ourselves that we are Christians but we do not have the Holy Spirit dwelling within us.

Everyone, then, who professes to be a Christian should ask himself, "Is there evidence of practical holiness in my life? Do I desire and strive after holiness? Do I grieve over my lack of it and earnestly seek the help of God to be holy?"

It is not those who profess to know Christ who will enter heaven, but those whose lives are holy. Even those who do "great Christian works" will not enter heaven unless they also do the will of God.

Jesus said,

"Not everyone who says to me, 'Lord, Lord,' will enter the kingdom of heaven, but only he who does the will of my Father who is in heaven.

"Many will say to me on that day, 'Lord, Lord, did we not prophesy in your name, and in your name drive out demons, and perform many miracles?' Then I will tell them plainly, 'I never knew you. Away from me, you evildoers!'" (Matthew 7:21-23)

SESSION TWO

Holiness Is Not an Option

(Chapter 3)

STUDY QUESTIONS

1. What do the following verses teach about our holy *standing* before God? (Note: The word *sanctified*, used in some Bible versions, means "made holy.")

   • Romans 5:19

   • Hebrews 10:10

   • 1 Peter 3:18

2. What do the following verses teach about holy *living*?

   • Ephesians 4:1,30

   • 1 Thessalonians 4:7

- Titus 2:11-12

3. Look up the verses below. From each one write a brief statement on why holiness is not optional for a Christian.

   - Psalm 66:18

   - Romans 8:13-14

   - 2 Timothy 2:21

   - 1 John 1:6

4. Consider Hebrews 12:14. What further efforts do you need to make toward holiness in your life?

5. *(For additional study)* Look up the following verses, analyzing what each one teaches about our holy standing before God and the need for holy living. Copy from your Bible the passages which are the most helpful to you, and explain why they are.

    •   Psalms 15:1-5; 32:3-4; Isaiah 64:6-7; Matthew 1:21; 7:21-23; 1 Corinthians 1:2; 2 Corinthians 5:17; Ephesians 1:4; James 2:14-26; 1 John 3:2-5

6. What application of the truths of this session do you want to make in your life?

The Holiness of Christ

Read the following portion of *The Pursuit of Holiness*. In the margins, record observations, illustrations, or questions that come to mind as you read. Then answer the study questions that follow the reading.

Chapter 4: The Holiness of Christ

God made him who had no sin to be sin for us, so that in him we might become the righteousness of God.
2 CORINTHIANS 5:21

Notes and Observations

Before speaking further of holiness in ourselves, it is well that we also consider the holiness of Christ. We need this first of all *to be firmly grounded in our security in Christ.* As we study more fully the implications of "Be holy because I am holy," we will see more of our own sinfulness. We will see the wickedness and deceitfulness of our hearts, and how far we miss the mark of God's perfect holiness. As this happens, the true Christian will in his heart flee for refuge in Christ. It is important therefore that we understand the righteousness of Christ, and the fact that His righteousness is credited to us.

On numerous occasions the Scriptures testify that Jesus during His time on earth lived a perfectly holy life. He is described as "without sin" (Hebrews 4:15); as One who "committed no sin" (1 Peter 2:22); and as "him who had no sin" (2 Corinthians 5:21). The apostle John stated, "In him is no sin" (1 John 3:5). The Old Testament describes Him prophetically as "the righteous servant" (Isaiah 53:11), and as One who "loved righteousness and hated wickedness" (Psalm 45:7). These statements, taken from six different writers of Scripture, show that the sinlessness of Jesus Christ is the universal teaching of the Bible.

Even more compelling, however, is Jesus' own testimony concerning Himself. On one occasion He looked the Pharisees squarely in the eye and asked, "Can any of you prove me guilty of sin?" (John 8:46). As someone has observed, it was not their failure to answer His question that is so significant, but the fact He dared to ask it. Here was Jesus in direct confrontation with people who hated Him. He had just told them they were of their father the devil, and that they wanted to carry out his desires. Surely if any people had a reason to point out to Him some careless act of His or some flaw of His character, they would. Furthermore, Jesus asked this question in the presence of His disciples, who lived with Him continuously and had ample opportunity to observe any inconsistencies. Yet Jesus dared to ask the question because He knew there was only one answer. He was without sin.

But the holiness of Jesus was more than simply the absence of actual sin. It was also a perfect conformity to the will of His Father. He stated that He came down from heaven "not to do my will but to do the will of him who sent me" (John 6:38). On another occasion, He said, "My food is to do the will of him who sent me" (John 4:34). Perhaps His highest testimony to His positive holiness was His statement, "I always do what pleases him" (John 8:29).

Such a positive declaration must include not only His actions but also His attitudes and motives. It is possible for us to do the right action from a wrong motive, but this does not please God. Holiness has to do with more than mere acts. Our motives must be holy, that is, arising from a desire to do something simply because it is the will of God. Our thoughts should be holy, since they are known to God even before they are formed in our minds. Jesus Christ perfectly met these standards, and He did it for us. He was born into this world subject to the law of God that He might fulfill it on our behalf (Galatians 4:4-5).

Whenever we seriously contemplate the holiness of God, our natural reaction is to say with Isaiah, "Woe is me, for I am ruined! Because I am a man of unclean lips, and I live among a people of unclean lips, and my eyes have seen the King, the Lord Almighty" (Isaiah 6:5).

A serious view of the holiness of God — His own moral perfection and infinite hatred of sin — will leave us, as it did Isaiah, seeing with utter dismay our own lack of holiness. His moral purity serves to magnify our impurity.

Therefore, it is important that we receive the same assurance that Isaiah received: "See . . . your guilt is taken away and your sin atoned for" (Isaiah 6:7). It is not only at the initial point of salvation that we need this assurance. In fact, the more we grow in holiness, the more we need assurance that the perfect righteousness of Christ is credited to us. This is true because a part of growing in holiness is the Holy Spirit's making us aware of our need of holiness. As we see this need, it is well for us to always keep in mind the righteousness of Jesus Christ on our behalf, and the fact that "God made him who had no sin to be sin for us, so that in him we might become the righteousness of God" (2 Corinthians 5:21).

The truth of our acceptance by God through the righteousness of Christ may seem so elementary that you wonder why it is stressed here. It is because we need to dwell on it to thwart the attacks of Satan. The Holy Spirit makes us more aware of our lack of holiness to stimulate us to deeper yearning and striving for holiness. But Satan will attempt to use the Holy Spirit's work to discourage us.

One of Satan's attacks is to try to convince you that you are not a genuine Christian after all. He will say something like, "A true Christian wouldn't think the evil thoughts you've been thinking today." Now it may be that six months ago Satan would not have come to you with such a suggestion because you were not troubled about your thoughts. But now that the Holy Spirit has begun to reveal how sinful your thoughts of lust and resentment and pride really are, you may begin to have doubts about your salvation.

A number of years ago, God was allowing me to go through

some deep inner struggles to teach me something of the sinfulness of my heart. During this time I was leading a weekly Bible study at a military base about an hour's drive from where I lived. Every Monday night as I left the fellowship of that Bible study and started my lonely drive home, Satan would begin to attack me: "How can anyone who is having the struggles you are having be a Christian?" he would ask. I began to fight him by resorting to an old gospel hymn, which begins,

> Just as I am, without one plea,
> But that Thy blood was shed for me,
> And that Thou bidst me come to Thee;
> O Lamb of God, I come.

I would sing through that hymn, and by the time I finished I would be praising God for His salvation given freely to me through Jesus Christ.

You, too, if you diligently pursue holiness, must often flee to the Rock of your salvation. You flee there, not to be saved again, but to confirm in your heart that you are saved through His righteousness alone. You begin to identify with Paul when he said, "Here is a trustworthy saying that deserves full acceptance: Christ Jesus came into the world to save sinners — of whom I am the worst" (1 Timothy 1:15). It is at this point that Christ's holy life lived on your behalf becomes so important to you.

A second reason we need to consider the holiness of Christ is because *His life is meant to be an example of holiness for us.* Peter told us that Christ left an example for us to follow in His steps (1 Peter 2:21). Peter spoke particularly of Christ's suffering without retaliation, but in the following verse he said also that Christ committed no sin. Paul urged us to be imitators of God (Ephesians 5:1), and also said "Follow my example, as I follow the example of Christ" (1 Corinthians 11:1).

Clearly then, the sinless holy life of Jesus Christ is meant to be an example for us. Consider then His statement, "I always do what pleases Him." Do we dare take that as our personal goal in life? Are we truly willing to scrutinize all our activities, all our goals and plans, and all of our impulsive actions in the light of this statement: "I am doing this to please God"?

If we ask that question honestly, we will begin to squirm a bit. We know we do some things, good things in themselves, to gain admiration for ourselves rather than glory for God. We do other things strictly for our own pleasure, without any regard for the glory of God.

What is my reaction when the neighborhood bully pesters my little boy? Usually my initial reaction comes from a spirit of retaliation till the Holy Spirit reminds me of the example of Jesus. How do we view those who do not show love for us? Do we see them as persons for whom Christ died or as persons who make our lives difficult?

I recall an unpleasant business encounter once with a person who later became a Christian through another's witness. When I learned of this, I was deeply chagrined to reflect on the fact that I had never once thought of him as a person for whom Christ died, but only as someone with whom I had an unpleasant experience. We need to learn to follow the example of Christ, who was moved with compassion for sinners and who could pray for them even as they nailed Him to the cross on Calvary.

In the words of nineteenth-century Scottish theologian John Brown, "Holiness does not consist in mystic speculations, enthusiastic fervours, or uncommanded austerities; it consists in thinking as God thinks, and willing as God wills."[1] Neither does holiness mean, as is so often thought, adhering to a list of "do's and don'ts," mostly don'ts. When Christ came into the world, He said, "I have come to do your will, O God" (Hebrews 10:7). This is the example we are to follow. In all of our thoughts, all of our actions, in every part of our character, the ruling principle that motivates and guides us should be the desire to follow Christ in doing the will of the Father. This is the high road we must follow in the pursuit of holiness.

The Holiness of Christ

(Chapter 4)

STUDY QUESTIONS

1. After studying the following verses, write a statement of what the holiness of Christ means to you in your personal pursuit of holiness.

   • Isaiah 6:5-7; Ephesians 5:1-2; 1 Timothy 1:15; 1 Peter 2:21

2. Look up the following verses about the holiness of Jesus Christ. Copy from your Bible those which are the most meaningful to you, and explain why they are.

   • Isaiah 53:11; John 8:29; 2 Corinthians 5:21; Hebrews 1:9; 4:15; 1 Peter 2:22; 1 John 3:5

3. If Satan questions your salvation with the thought, "A true Christian wouldn't think the evil thoughts you've been thinking today," how should you respond?

4. *(For additional study)* Look up the following verses about the holiness of Christ. Which are the most significant to you? Why?

   • John 4:34; 6:38; 8:45-49; Hebrews 10:7; 1 Peter 1:18-19

5. What application of the truths of this session do you want to make in your life?

The Battle for Holiness

Read the following portion of *The Pursuit of Holiness*. In the margins, record observations, illustrations, or questions that come to mind as you read. Then answer the study questions that follow the reading.

Chapter 5: A Change of Kingdoms

For we know that our old self was crucified with him so that the body of sin might be rendered powerless, that we should no longer be slaves to sin because anyone who has died has been freed from sin.
ROMANS 6:6-7, NASB

Many Christians have a basic desire to live a holy life, but have come to believe they simply cannot do it. They have struggled for years with particular sins or deficiencies of character. While not living in gross sin, they have more or less given up ever attaining a life of holiness and have settled down to a life of moral mediocrity with which neither they nor God are pleased. The promise of Romans 6:6-7 seems impossibly beyond them. The strong commands of Scripture to live a consistently holy life only frustrate them.

Many have sought to live a holy life by their own willpower; others have sought it solely by faith. Many have agonized in prayer over particular sins, seemingly without success. Scores of books have been written to help us discover the "secret" of the "victorious life."

In our search for answers to our sin problems, a troublesome question arises: "What should I look to God for and what am I responsible for myself?" Many are confused at this point. When we first start to live the Christian life, we confidently assume we will simply discover from the Bible what God wants us to do and start doing it. We fail to reckon with our tendency to cling to our old sinful ways.

After experiencing a great deal of failure with our sinful nature, we are told that we have been trying to live the Christian life in the energy of the flesh. We need to "stop trying and start trusting," or to "let go and let God." We are told that if we just turn our sin problem over to Christ and rest in His finished work on Calvary, He will then live His life in us and we will experience a life of victory over sin.

Having experienced failure and frustration with our sin problem, we are delighted to be told that God has already done it all and that we only need to rest in Christ's finished work. After struggling with our sins to the point of despair, this new idea is like a life preserver to a drowning man, almost like hearing the gospel for the first time.

But after a while, if we are truly honest with ourselves, we discover we are still experiencing defeat at the hands of our sinful natures. The victory seemingly promised us still eludes us. We still struggle with pride, jealousy, materialism, impatience, and lust. We still eat too much, waste our time, criticize each other, shade the truth just a little, and indulge in a dozen other sins, all the time hating ourselves for doing them.

Then we wonder what is wrong. "Why can't I," we ask ourselves, "experience the victory described in all the books that others seem to have experienced?" We begin to feel that something is uniquely wrong with us, that somehow our sinful natures must be worse than others. Then we begin to despair.

Years ago a fellow Christian warned me that Satan would try to confuse us on the issue of what God has done for us and what we must do ourselves. I have come to see the insight he had in making that statement. Lack of understanding on that issue has led to great confusion in our pursuit of holiness. It is very important that we make this distinction; for God has indeed made provision for us to live a holy life, but He also has given us definite responsibilities.

Let us first look at God's provision for us.

In the Bible we read, "Therefore, do not let sin reign in your mortal body so that you obey its evil desires" (Romans 6:12). The first thing we should notice in this passage is that the pursuit of holiness — this not allowing sin to reign in our mortal bodies — is something *we* have to do. Paul's statement is one of exhortation. He addressed himself to our wills. He said, "Do not let sin reign," implying that this is something for which we ourselves are responsible. The experience of holiness is not a gift we receive like justification, but something which we are clearly exhorted to work at.

The second thing to note from Paul's exhortation is that it is based on what he had just said. Note the connecting word *therefore*. Clearly he meant to say something like, "In view of what I have just said, do not let sin reign in your mortal body." To state it another way, we are to pursue holiness because certain facts are true.

What are these facts?

Let us take a look at Romans 6. In answer to the question "Shall we go on sinning so that grace may increase?" Paul said, "We died to sin; how can we live in it any longer?" (verses 1-2). Then Paul developed that idea (verses 3-11). It is evident that the word *therefore* (verse 12) refers back to this fact that we died to sin. Because we died to sin, we are not to let it reign in our mortal bodies.

If we are to obey the exhortation of verse 12, it is vital that we understand what Paul means by the expression *we died to sin*. As we read this passage, the first thing we observe is that our dying to sin is the result of our union with Christ (verses 2-11). Because He died to sin, we died to sin. Therefore, it is apparent that our dying to sin is not something we do, but something Christ has done, the value of which accrues to all who are united with Him.

The second observation we can make is that our dying to

sin is a fact whether we realize it or not. Because Christ died to sin, all who are united with Him died to sin. Our dying to sin is not something we do, or something we make come true in our experience by reckoning it to be so. Some have misunderstood this point. We have gotten the idea that to have died to sin means to somehow be removed from sin's ability to touch us. However, to experience this in our daily lives we are told we must *reckon* ourselves dead to sin (verse 11, KJV). We are further told that if we are not experiencing victory over our besetting sins, it is because we are not reckoning on the fact that we died to sin.

We are indeed to reckon — or to count or consider — ourselves dead to sin, but our reckoning does not make it true, even in our experience. Verses 11 and 12 must be taken together. Because we are dead to sin through our union with Christ, we are not to let sin reign in our mortal bodies. Our daily experience with regard to sin is determined — not by our reckoning, but by our will — by whether we allow sin to reign in our bodies. But our will must be influenced by the fact that we died to sin.

What then does Paul mean by his expression *died to sin*? He means we died to the dominion of sin, or to the reign of sin. Before we trusted in Jesus Christ for our salvation, we were in the kingdom of Satan and sin. We "followed the ways of this world and of the ruler of the kingdom of the air [the devil]" (Ephesians 2:2). We were under the power of Satan (Acts 26:18) and the dominion of darkness (Colossians 1:13). Paul said we were slaves of sin (Romans 6:17). We were born into this kingdom of sin, slavery, and death. Every person who has ever lived since Adam, except for the incarnate Son of God, has been born a slave in the kingdom of sin and Satan.

But through our union with Christ we have died to this realm of sin. We have been set free from sin (Romans 6:18), rescued from the dominion of darkness (Colossians 1:13), and turned from the power of Satan to God (Acts 26:18). Before our salvation we were in bondage to sin, under the reign and rule of sin. Regardless of how decent and moral we were, we lived in the kingdom of sin. But now through our union with Christ in His death to sin, we have been delivered out of the realm of sin and placed in the kingdom and realm of righteousness.[1]

Professor John Murray, in commenting on the clause *we died to sin*, said,

> If we view sin as a realm or sphere, then the believer no longer lives in that realm or sphere. And just as it is true with reference to life in the sphere of this world that the person who has died 'passed away, and lo, he was not: yea, I sought him, but he could not be found' (Psalm 37:36), so it is with the sphere of sin; the believer is no longer there because he has died to sin. . . . The believer died to sin once and he has been translated to another realm.[2]

It is because we were in this realm of sin, under its reign and rule, that we began to sin from infancy. Because we were slaves, we acted like slaves. We developed sinful habits and a sinful character. Even if we were what the world considers "good," we lived for ourselves, not for God. Our attitude toward Christ was expressed by the words of His enemies: "We don't want this man to be our king" (Luke 19:14).

But if we have been delivered from this realm, why do we still sin? Though God has delivered us from the reign of sin, our sinful natures still reside within us. Even though sin's dominion and rule are broken, the remaining sin that dwells in believers exerts a tremendous power, constantly working toward evil.

An illustration from warfare can help us see how this is true. In a particular nation two competing factions were fighting for control of the country. Eventually, with the help of an outside army, one faction won the war and assumed control of the nation's government. But the losing side did not stop fighting. They simply changed their tactics to guerrilla warfare and continued to fight. In fact, they were so successful that the country supplying the outside help could not withdraw its troops.

So it is with the Christian. Satan has been defeated and the reign of sin overthrown. But our sinful natures resort to a sort of guerrilla warfare to lead us into sin. This results in the struggle between the Spirit and our sinful natures which Paul wrote about: "For the sinful nature desires what is contrary to the Spirit, and the Spirit what is contrary to the sinful nature. They are in conflict with each other, so that you do not do what you want" (Galatians 5:17).

Further, because we are born as sinners, we have from birth developed habits of sin. As Jay Adams says, "We were born sinners, but it took practice to develop our particular styles of sinning. The old life was disciplined [trained] toward ungodliness."[3] We all tend to act according to these sinful habits that have been engraved in us from long practice.

Suppose, for example, I had a lame leg and as a result developed a limp. If through surgery my lameness is cured, I would still tend to limp out of habit. Or do you suppose that when slaves were freed by President Lincoln's Emancipation Proclamation, they immediately began to think as free men? Undoubtedly they still tended to act as slaves because they had developed habit patterns of slavery.

In a similar manner, Christians tend to sin out of habit. It is our habit to look out for ourselves instead of others, to retaliate when injured in some way, and to indulge the appetites of our bodies. It is our habit to live for ourselves and not for God. When we become Christians, we do not drop all this overnight. In fact, we will spend the rest of our lives putting off these habits and putting on habits of holiness.

Not only have we been slaves to sin, but we still live in a world populated by slaves of sin. The conventional values around us reflect this slavery, and the world tries to conform us to its own sinful mold.

Therefore, though sin no longer reigns in us, it will constantly try to get at us. Though we have been delivered from the kingdom of sin and its rule, we have not been delivered from its attacks. As Dr. Martin Lloyd-Jones says in his exposition of Romans 6, though sin cannot reign in us, that is, in our essential personality, it can, if left unchecked, reign in our mortal bodies.[4] It will turn the natural instincts of our bodies into lust. It will turn our natural appetites into indulgence, our need for clothing and shelter into materialism, and our normal sexual interest into immorality.

That is why Paul exhorted us to be on our guard so that we will not let sin reign in our bodies. Before our salvation, before our death to the reign of sin, such an exhortation would have been futile. You cannot say to a slave, "Live as a free man," but you can say that to someone delivered from slavery. Now that we are in fact dead to sin — to its rule and reign — we are to count on that as being true. We are to keep before us this fact that we are no longer slaves. We can now stand up to sin and say no to it. Before we had no choice; now we have one. When we sin as Christians, we do not sin as slaves, but as individuals with the freedom of choice. We sin because we choose to sin.

To summarize then, we have been set free from the reign and rule of sin, the kingdom of unrighteousness. Our deliverance is through our union with Christ in His death. When Christ entered this world He voluntarily entered the realm of sin, though He never sinned. When He died, He died to this realm of sin (Romans 6:10), and through our union with Him we died to this realm also. We are to count on this fact that we are dead to sin's rule, that we can stand up to it and say no. Therefore we are to guard our bodies so that sin does not reign in us.

So we see that God has made provision for our holiness. Through Christ He has delivered us from sin's reign so that we now can resist sin. But the responsibility for resisting is ours. God does not do that for us. To confuse the *potential* for resisting (which God provided) with the *responsibility* for resisting (which is ours) is to court disaster in our pursuit of holiness.

Chapter 6: The Battle for Holiness
*So I find this law at work: When I want
to do good, evil is right there with me.*
ROMANS 7:21

Through our union with Christ in His death we are delivered from the dominion of sin. But we still find sin struggling to gain mastery over us, as Paul depicted so vividly: "When I want to do good, evil is right there with me" (Romans 7:21). We may not like the fact that we have this lifelong struggle with sin, but the more we realize and accept it, the better equipped we will be to deal with it. The more we discover about the strength of indwelling sin, the less we feel its effects. To the extent that we discover this law of sin within ourselves, we will abhor and fight against it.

But though believers still have this indwelling propensity to sin, the Holy Spirit maintains within us a prevailing desire for holiness (1 John 3:9). The believer struggles with the sin God enables him to see in himself. This is the picture we see in Romans 7:21, and it distinguishes believers from unbelievers who lie serenely content in their darkness.

Interpretations of Romans 7:14-25 fall into three basic groups. It is not the purpose of this book to discuss those interpretations or to decide in favor of one of them. Whatever our interpretation of Romans 7, all Christians acknowledge the universal application of Paul's statement, "When I want to do good, evil is right there with me."

As indicated in the previous chapter, indwelling sin remains in us even though it has been dethroned. And though it has been overthrown and weakened, its nature has not changed. Sin is still hostile to God and cannot submit to His law (Romans 8:7). Thus we have an implacable enemy of righteousness right in our own hearts. What diligence and watchfulness is required of us when this enemy in our souls is ready to oppose every effort to do good!

If we are to wage a successful war against this enemy within, it is important that we know something of its nature and tactics. First of all, the Scripture indicates that *the seat of indwelling sin is the heart*. "For from within, out of men's hearts, come evil thoughts, sexual immorality, theft, murder, adultery, greed, malice, deceit, lewdness, envy, slander, arrogance, and folly. All these evils come from inside and make a man 'unclean'" (Mark 7:21-23; see also Genesis 6:5 and Luke 6:45).

The word *heart* in Scripture is used in various ways. Sometimes it means our reason or understanding, sometimes our affections and emotions, and sometimes our will. Generally it denotes the whole soul of man and all its faculties, not individually, but as they all work together in doing good or evil. The mind as it reasons, discerns, and judges; the emotions as they like or dislike; the conscience as it determines and warns; and the will as it chooses or refuses — are all together called the heart.[5]

The Bible tells us that the heart is deceitful and unsearchable to any but God alone (Jeremiah 17:9-10). Even as believers we do not know our own hearts (1 Corinthians 4:3-5). None of us can discern fully the hidden motives, the secret intrigues, the windings and turnings of his heart. And in this unsearchable heart dwells the law of sin. Much of sin's strength lies in this, that we fight with an enemy we cannot fully search out.

The heart is also deceitful. It excuses, rationalizes, and justifies our actions. It blinds us to entire areas of sin in our lives. It causes us to deal with sin using only halfway measures, or to think that mental assent to the Word of God is the same as obedience (James 1:22).

Knowing that indwelling sin occupies a heart that is deceitful and unsearchable should make us extremely wary. We need to ask God daily to search our hearts for sin that we cannot or will not see. This was David's prayer: "Search me, O God, and know my heart; test me and know my anxious thoughts. See if there is any offensive way in me, and lead me in the way everlasting" (Psalm 139:23-24). God's primary means of searching our hearts this way is through His Word, as we read it under the power of the Holy Spirit. "The word of God is living and active. Sharper than any double-edged sword, it penetrates even to dividing soul and spirit, joints and marrow; it judges the thoughts and attitudes of the heart" (Hebrews 4:12). As we pray for God to search our hearts, we must continually expose ourselves to the searching of His Word.

We must be careful to let the Holy Spirit do this searching. If we try to search our own hearts, we are apt to fall into one or both of two traps. The first is the trap of morbid introspection. Introspection can easily become the tool of Satan, who is called the "accuser" (Revelation 12:10). One of his chief weapons is discouragement. He knows that if he can make us discouraged and dispirited, we will not fight the battle for holiness.

The second trap is that of missing the real issues in our lives. The deceitfulness of Satan and of our own hearts will lead us to focus on secondary issues. I recall a young man who came to talk to me about a sin problem in his life over which he had no control. But though this problem loomed overwhelmingly in his mind, there were other areas of need in his life to which he was blind. The sin he saw was hurting only himself, but the problems he didn't see were hurting others every day. Only the Holy Spirit can enable us to see such areas to which we are blind.

The seat of indwelling sin, then, is our deceitful, unsearchable heart. A second thing we should realize is that *indwelling sin works largely through our desires.* Ever since his fall in the Garden of Eden, man has listened to his desires more than his reason. Desire has come to be the strongest faculty of man's heart.[6] The next time you face one of your typical temptations, watch for the struggle between your desires and your reason. If you give

54

in to temptation, it will be because desire has overcome reason in the struggle to influence your will. The world recognizes this and makes appeals to our desires through what the writer of Hebrews calls "the pleasures of sin" (Hebrews 11:25).

Not all desire is evil, of course. Paul speaks of his desire to know Christ (Philippians 3:10), of his desire for the salvation of his fellow Jews (Romans 10:1), and the desire that his spiritual children grow to maturity (Galatians 4:19).

We are speaking here, however, about the evil desires that lead us into sin. James said we are tempted when we are dragged away and enticed by our own evil desires (James 1:14). If we are to win this battle for holiness, we must recognize that the basic problem lies within us. It is our own evil desires that lead us into temptation. We may think we merely respond to outward temptations that are presented to us. But the truth is, our evil desires are constantly searching out temptations to satisfy their insatiable lusts. Consider the particular temptations to which you are especially vulnerable, and note how often you find yourself searching out occasions to satisfy those evil desires.

Even when we are engaged in one way or another with the battle against a particular sin, our evil desire, or indwelling sin, will lead us into playing with that very sin. Sometimes while confessing a sin we find ourselves starting once again to dwell on the evil thoughts associated with that sin, and we may be tempted again.

There are also, of course, many occasions when we encounter temptation unexpectedly. When this happens our evil desires are ready and prompt to receive and embrace them. Just as fire burns any combustible material presented to it, so our own evil desires immediately respond to temptation. John Owen said that sin carries on its war by entangling our affections (what I have here called desires) and drawing them away. Hence, said Owen, denying sin must be chiefly directed on the affections. We must make sure our desires are directed toward glorifying God, he said, and not satisfying the lusts of our bodies.[7]

55

The third thing we must understand about indwelling sin is that *it tends to deceive our understanding or reasoning.* Our reason, enlightened by the Holy Spirit through the Word of God, stands in the way of sin gaining mastery over us through our desires. Therefore Satan's great strategy is to deceive our minds. Paul spoke of the "deceitful desires" of the old self (Ephesians 4:22). He said that we were at one time "deceived and enslaved by all kinds of passions and pleasures" (Titus 3:3). These passages speak of our old life, but we must realize that this deceit still wages war against us, though it no longer has mastery over us.

Deceit of the mind is carried on by degrees, little by little. We are first drawn away from watchfulness, then from obedience. We become like Ephraim, of whom God said, "Foreigners sap his strength, but he does not realize it. His hair is sprinkled with gray, but he does not notice" (Hosea 7:9). We are drawn away from watchfulness by overconfidence. We come to believe we are beyond a particular temptation. We look at someone else's fall and say, "I would never do that." But Paul warned us, "If you think you are standing firm, be careful that you don't fall" (1 Corinthians 10:12). Even when helping a fallen brother, we are to watch ourselves lest we also be tempted (Galatians 6:1).

We are often drawn away from obedience by the abuse of grace. Jude speaks of certain men "who change the grace of our God into a license for immorality" (Jude 4). We abuse grace when we think we can sin and then receive forgiveness by claiming 1 John 1:9. We abuse grace when, after sinning, we dwell on the compassion and mercy of God to the exclusion of His holiness and hatred of sin.

We are drawn away from obedience when we begin to question what God says in His Word. This was Satan's first tactic with Eve (Genesis 3:1-5). Just as he said to Eve, "You surely shall not die!" so he says to us, "It is just a little thing!" or "God will not judge that sin."

So we see that though sin no longer has dominion over us, it wages its guerrilla warfare against us. If left unchecked, it will

SESSION FOUR: The Battle for Holiness

defeat us. Our recourse against this warfare is to deal swiftly and firmly with the first motions of indwelling sin. If temptation finds any lodging place in the soul, it will use that to lead us into sin. "When the sentence for a crime is not quickly carried out, the hearts of the people are filled with schemes to do wrong" (Ecclesiastes 8:11).

Furthermore, we must never consider that our fight against sin is at an end. The heart is unsearchable, our evil desires are insatiable, and our reason is constantly in danger of being deceived. Well did Jesus say, "Watch and pray so that you will not fall into temptation" (Matthew 26:41). And Solomon warned us, "Above all else, guard your heart, for it is the wellspring of life" (Proverbs 4:23).

The Battle for Holiness

(Chapters 5 and 6)

STUDY QUESTIONS

1. Study Romans 6:1-12 and Colossians 1:13. In your own words, what does it mean to have died to sin?

2. What does each of the following verses teach about our hearts and sin?

   • Jeremiah 17:9-10

   • Mark 7:21-23

   • Romans 7:18

3. Using the following verses, explain the nature of our desires and why we need to watch them closely.

    *   Ephesians 4:20-22; Titus 3:3; James 1:14-15

4. *(For additional study)* Look up the following verses about our struggle against sin, write down those which are the most helpful to you, and explain why they are.

    *   Genesis 6:5-6; Psalm 139:23-24; Proverbs 4:23; Luke 6:45; Acts 26:18; Romans 6:17-23; 1 Corinthians 10:12; Galatians 5:17; 6:1; Hebrews 4:12; James 1:22; 1 John 3:9

5. Why, if we died to sin, do we still sin?

6. As those who have died to sin, what is our responsibility with regard to sin now?

7. What application of the truths of this session do you want to make in your own life?

God's Provision and Our Responsibility

Read the following portion of *The Pursuit of Holiness*. In the margins, record observations, illustrations, or questions that come to mind as you read. Then answer the study questions that follow the reading.

Chapter 7: Help in the Daily Battle

*In the same way count yourselves dead
to sin but alive to God in Christ Jesus.*
ROMANS 6:11

Notes and Observations

In the last session (chapter 5) we saw how God has delivered us from the realm and reign of sin through union with Christ in His death. We were slaves to sin and in slavery we committed sins. We developed sinful habits regardless of how "good" we were. But Jesus Christ came into this sinful world and took our place on Calvary. He died to sin and through our union with Him we died to sin also. Now we are freed from sin's reign; we are no longer its slaves. We are to count on this fact and resist sin so that it does not reign in our mortal bodies.

In chapter 6 we saw how sin still lives within us, waging its "guerrilla warfare" through evil desires and deceiving our minds. It may well seem that whatever hope for holiness was held out in chapter 5 was effectively taken away in chapter 6. "What good does it do," you may ask, "to be told that the war with sin was won by Christ in His death on the cross if I am still harassed and often defeated by sin in my heart?"

To experience practical, everyday holiness, we must accept the fact that God in His infinite wisdom has seen fit to allow this daily battle with indwelling sin. But God does not leave us to do battle alone. Just as He delivered us from the overall reign of sin, so He has made ample provision for us to win the daily skirmishes against sin.

This brings us to the second point in Romans 6:11 that we are to count on and keep before us. We are not only dead to sin, as we saw in chapter 5, we also are alive to God. We have not only been delivered from the dominion of darkness, we also have been brought into the kingdom of Christ. Paul said we have become slaves of righteousness (Romans 6:18). God does not leave us suspended in a state of neutrality. He delivers us from sin's reign into the reign of His Son.

What is the significance of being alive unto God? How does it help us in our pursuit of holiness? For one thing, it means *we are united with Christ in all His power.* It is certainly true we cannot live a holy life in our own strength. Christianity is not a do-it-yourself thing.

Notice the attitude of the apostle Paul in Philippians 4:11-13. He is talking about how he has learned to be content whatever the circumstances, whether plenty or want, whether well-fed or hungry. He says he can respond this way through Christ, who gives him strength. How does this apply to holiness? Our reactions to circumstances are a part of our walk of holiness. Holiness is not a series of do's and don'ts, but conformity to the character of God and obedience to the will of God. Accepting with contentment whatever circumstances God allows for me is very much a part of a holy walk.

But notice that Paul said he could respond in contentment because Christ gave the strength to do so. We see this again where Paul said he prayed that the Colossians would be "strengthened with all power according to his glorious might so that you may have great endurance and patience" (Colossians 1:11). Where do endurance and patience come from? They come as we are strengthened with God's power.

Consider again another prayer Paul described in his letter to the Ephesians. He said he was praying for them "that out of his glorious riches he may strengthen you with *power* through his

Spirit in your inner being" (Ephesians 3:16, emphasis added). He concluded the prayer by acknowledging that God "is able to do immeasurably more than all we ask or imagine, according to his *power* that is at work within us" (3:20, emphasis added).

This is the first implication we should grasp of being "alive unto God." We are united with the One who is at work in us to strengthen us with His mighty power. We have all known the awful sense of hopelessness caused by sin's power. We have resolved scores of times never to give in again to a particular temptation, and yet we do. Then Satan comes to us and says, "You might as well give up. You can never overcome that sin." It is true that in ourselves we cannot. But we are alive to God, united to Him who will strengthen us. By reckoning on this fact — counting it to be true — we will experience the strength we need to fight that temptation.

Only as we reckon on these twin facts — that I am dead to sin and its reign over me and that I am alive to God, united to Him who strengthens me — can I keep sin from reigning in my mortal body.

Dr. Martyn Lloyd-Jones says, "To realize this takes away from us that old sense of hopelessness which we have all known and felt because of the terrible power of sin. . . . How does it work? It works in this way: I lose my sense of hopelessness because I can say to myself that not only am I no longer under the dominion of sin, but I am under the dominion of another power that nothing can frustrate. However weak I may be, it is the power of God that is working in me."[1]

This is not theoretical teaching, something to be placed on the library shelves of our minds and admired, but of no practical value in the battle for holiness. To count on the fact that we are dead to sin and alive to God is something we must do actively.

To do it we must *form the habit* of continually realizing that we are dead to sin and alive to God. Practically speaking, we do this when, by faith in God's Word, we resist sin's advances and temptations. We count on the fact that we are alive to God when by faith we look to Christ for the power we need to do the resisting. Faith, however, must always be based on fact, and Romans 6:11 is a fact for us.

A second implication of being alive to God is that *He has given us His Holy Spirit to live within us*. Actually this is not a second result, but another way of looking at our union with Christ, for His Spirit is the agent of this union. It is He who gives spiritual life and the strength to live that life (Romans 8:9-11). It is the Spirit of God who works in us that we may decide and act according to God's good purpose (Philippians 2:13).

Paul said, "God did not call us to be impure, but to live a holy life. Therefore, he who rejects this instruction does not reject man but God, who gives you his Holy Spirit" (1 Thessalonians 4:7-8). Here Paul connects the giving of the Holy Spirit with our living a holy life. He is called the Holy Spirit, and He is sent primarily to make us holy — to conform us to the character of God. The connection of these two thoughts, the Holy Spirit and a holy life, is also found in other passages. For example, we are told to flee sexual immorality because our bodies are temples of the Holy Spirit (1 Corinthians 6:18-19). We are also told that we are controlled not by our sinful nature but by the Spirit, if the Spirit of God lives in us (Romans 8:9). We read, "Live by the Spirit, and you will not gratify the desires of the sinful nature" (Galatians 5:16).

Why do we have the Holy Spirit living within us to strengthen us toward holiness? It is because we are alive to God. We are now living under the reign of God, who unites us to Christ and gives us His Holy Spirit to dwell within us.[2]

The Holy Spirit strengthens us to holiness first by enabling us to see our need of holiness. He enlightens our understanding so that we begin to see God's standard of holiness. Then He causes us to become aware of our specific areas of sin. One of Satan's most powerful weapons is making us spiritually blind — unable to see our sinful character. The Bible says, "The heart is deceitful above all things and beyond cure. Who can understand it?" (Jeremiah 17:9). No one can understand it and expose it except the Holy Spirit.

Even Christians taking in the teaching of the Bible can be deceived about their own sins. We somehow feel that consent to the teaching of Scripture is equivalent to obedience. We may hear a point of application in a sermon or perhaps discover it in our own personal Bible reading or study. We say, "Yes that is true; that is something I need to act on." But we let it drop at that point. James says when we do that, we deceive ourselves (James 1:22).

As we grow in the Christian life we face increasing danger of spiritual pride. We know the correct doctrines, the right methods and the proper do's and don'ts. But we may not see the poverty of our own spiritual character. We may not see our critical and unforgiving spirit, our habit of backbiting, or our tendency to judge others. We may become like the Laodiceans of whom our Lord said, "You say, 'I am rich; I have acquired wealth and do not need a thing.' But you do not realize that you are wretched, pitiful, poor, blind, and naked" (Revelation 3:17).

David was like this when he committed adultery with Bathsheba and then had her husband murdered to cover his first sin (2 Samuel 12:1-13). Was he repentant and humbled over his despicable acts? Not at all. In fact, he was ready to judge another man for a far lesser crime and to condemn him to death (verse 5). How could he do this? Because he was spiritually blind. It was not till Nathan the prophet said to David, "You are the man!" that David was able to see the awful heinousness of his crime.

It is the Holy Spirit's ministry to make us see that we are poverty-stricken because of our sins. He comes to us and says, "You are the man!" Even though such a message may come from the loving, caring lips of a brother in Christ, it is the Holy Spirit who enables us to accept it and to say as David did, "I have sinned against the Lord." The Holy Spirit opens the inner recesses of our hearts and enables us to see the moral cesspools hidden there. This is where He begins His ministry of making us holy.

The natural result of seeing God's standard and our sinfulness is the awakening within us of a desire to be holy. This is also the ministry of the Holy Spirit as He works to make us holy. We are sorry for our sins with a godly sorrow that leads to repentance (2 Corinthians 7:10). We say with David, "Wash away all my iniquity, and cleanse me from my sin. . . . Cleanse me with hyssop, and I will be clean; wash me, and I will be whiter than snow" (Psalm 51:2,7).

Paul said, "For it is God who works in you to will and to act according to his good purpose" (Philippians 2:13). Before we can *act* we must *will*. To will means to desire and resolve. When the Holy Spirit shows us our sinfulness, He does not do this to lead us to despair but to lead us to holiness. He does this by creating within us a hatred of our sins and a desire for holiness.

Only one who has a strong desire to be holy will ever persevere in the painfully slow and difficult task of pursuing holiness. There are too many failures. The habits of our old nature and the attacks of Satan are too strong for us to persevere unless the Holy Spirit is at work in us to create a desire for holiness.

The Holy Spirit creates this desire, not only by showing us our sins, but also by showing us God's standard of holiness. He does this through the Scriptures. As we read and study the Scriptures or hear them taught, we are captivated by the moral beauty of God's standard of holiness. Even though His standard may seem far beyond us, we recognize and respond to that which is "holy, righteous, and good" (Romans 7:12). Even though we fail so often, in our inner being we "delight in God's law" (Romans 7:22).

Here then is another distinction we must make between what God does and what we must do. If the Holy Spirit uses Scripture to show us our need and to stimulate a desire for holiness, then doesn't it follow that we must be in God's Word on a consistent basis? Should we not go to the Word, whether to hear it preached or to do our own study, with the prayer that the Holy Spirit would search our hearts for any sin in us? (Psalm 139:23-24).

After the Holy Spirit has enabled us to see our need and created within us a desire for holiness, there remains something more that He must do. He must give us the spiritual strength to live a holy life. Paul said, "Live by the Spirit, and you will not gratify the desires of the sinful nature" (Galatians 5:16). To live by the Spirit is to live both in obedience *to* and dependence *on* the Holy Spirit. There is a balance then between our wills (expressed by obedience) and our faith (expressed by our dependence). But at this point we are considering the aspect of our dependence on the Holy Spirit.

No one overcomes the corruptions of his heart except by the enabling strength of the Spirit of God. Peter said that God has given us "His very great and precious promises, so that through them you may participate in the divine nature and escape the corruption in the world" (2 Peter 1:4). Through participation in the divine nature we escape corruption — and this participation is through the indwelling Holy Spirit.

We express our dependence on the Holy Spirit for a holy life in two ways. The first is through *a humble and consistent intake of the Scripture*. If we truly desire to live in the realm of the Spirit we must continually feed our minds with His truth. It is hypocritical to pray for victory over our sins yet be careless in our intake of the Word of God.

It is possible, though, to be consistent in our intake of the Word of God without an attitude of dependence on the Holy Spirit. God says, "This is the one I esteem: he who is humble and contrite in spirit, and trembles at my word" (Isaiah 66:2). We are to come to the Word in a spirit of humility and contrition because we recognize that we are sinful, that we are often blind to our sinfulness, and that we need the enlightening power of the Holy Spirit in our hearts.

The second way we express our dependence on the Spirit is *to pray for holiness*. The apostle Paul prayed continually for the working of God's Spirit in the lives of those to whom he was writing. He told the Ephesians that he prayed God would "strengthen you with power through his Spirit in your inner being" (Ephesians 3:16). He prayed that God would fill the Colossians "with the knowledge of his will through all spiritual wisdom and understanding" so that they might "live a life worthy of the Lord and may please him in every way" (Colossians 1:9-10).

He wrote to the Thessalonians, "May God Himself, the God of peace, sanctify you [make you holy] through and through" (1 Thessalonians 5:23); and, "May the Lord make your love increase and overflow for each other and for everyone else. . . . May he strengthen your hearts so that you will be blameless and holy in the presence of our God" (1 Thessalonians 3:12-13). Clearly the apostle Paul knew we depend on the Holy Spirit for holiness, and he expressed this dependence through prayer.

As a young Christian I had the idea that all I had to do to live a holy life was to find out from the Bible what God wanted me to do and go do it. Christians with maturity will smile at this naive assumption, but I see younger Christians starting off with the same air of self-confidence. We have to learn that we are dependent upon the enabling power of the Holy Spirit to attain any degree of holiness. Then, as we look to Him, we will see Him working in us — revealing our sin, creating a desire for holiness, and giving us the strength to respond to Him in obedience.

Chapter 8: Obedience — Not Victory

For if you live according to the sinful nature, you
will die; but if by the Spirit you put to death
the misdeeds of the body, you will live.
ROMANS 8:13

God has made provision for our holiness and He has also given us a responsibility for it. As we saw in chapters 5 and 7, God's provision for us consists in delivering us from the reign of sin, uniting us with Christ, and giving us the indwelling Holy Spirit to reveal sin, to create a desire for holiness, and to strengthen us in our pursuit of holiness. Through the power of the Holy Spirit and according to the new nature He gives, we are to put to death the misdeeds of the body (Romans 8:13).

Though it is the Spirit who enables us to put to death our corruptions, yet Paul says this is our action as well. The very same work is from one point of view the work of the Spirit, and from another the work of man.

In the previous chapter we emphasized the "by the Spirit" part of this verse. In this chapter we want to look at our responsibility — "you put to death the misdeeds of the body."

It is clear from this passage that God puts responsibility for living a holy life squarely on us. We are to do something. We are not to "stop trying and start trusting"; we are to put to death the misdeeds of the body. Over and over again in the epistles — not only Paul's, but the other apostles' as well — we are commanded to assume our responsibility for a holy walk. Paul exhorted, "Put to death, therefore, whatever belongs to your earthly nature" (Colossians 3:5). This is something we are told to do.

The writer of Hebrews said, "Therefore, since we are surrounded by such a great cloud of witnesses, let us throw off everything that hinders and the sin that so easily entangles, and let us run with perseverance the race marked out for us" (Hebrews 12:1). He says *let us* throw off the sin and *let us* run with perseverance. Clearly he expects us to assume responsibility for running the Christian race. James said, "Submit yourselves, then, to God. Resist the devil, and he will flee from you" (James 4:7). It is we who are to submit to God and resist the devil. This is our responsibility. Peter said, "Make every effort to be found spotless, blameless and at peace with him" (2 Peter 3:14). The clause *make every effort* addresses itself to our wills. It is something we must decide to do.

During a certain period in my Christian life, I thought that any effort on my part to live a holy life was "of the flesh" and that "the flesh profits for nothing." I thought God would not bless any effort on my part to live the Christian life, just as He would not bless any effort on my part to become a Christian by good works. Just as I received Christ Jesus by faith, so I was to seek a holy life only by faith. Any effort on my part was just getting in God's way. I misapplied the statement, "You will not have to fight this battle. Take up your positions; stand firm and see the deliverance the Lord will give you" (2 Chronicles 20:17), to mean that I was just to turn it all over to the Lord and He would fight the sin in my life. In fact, in the margin of the Bible I was using during that period, I wrote alongside the verse these words: "Illustration of walking in the Spirit."

How foolish I was. I misconstrued dependence on the Holy Spirit to mean I was to make no effort, that I had no responsibility. I mistakenly thought if I turned it all over to the Lord, He would make my choices for me and would choose obedience over disobedience. All I needed was to look to Him for holiness. But this is not God's way. He makes provision for our holiness, but He gives us the responsibility of using those provisions.

The Holy Spirit has been given to all Christians. Dr. Martyn Lloyd-Jones says,

> The Holy Spirit is in us; He is working in us, and empowering us, giving us the ability. . . . This is the New Testament teaching — "Work out your own salvation with fear and trembling." We have to do so. But note the accompaniment — "Because it is God that worketh in you, both to will and to do of His good pleasure"! The Holy Spirit is working in us "both to will and to do." It is because I am not left to myself, it is because I am not "absolutely hopeless," since the Spirit is in me, that I am exhorted to work out my own salvation with fear and trembling.[3]

We must rely on the Spirit in our putting to death the deeds of the body. As Lloyd-Jones observes in his exposition of Romans

8:13, it is the Holy Spirit who "differentiates Christianity from morality, from 'legalism' and false Puritanism."[4] But our reliance on the Spirit is not intended to foster an attitude of "I can't do it," but one of "I can do it through Him who strengthens me." The Christian should never complain of want of ability and power. If we sin, it is because we choose to sin, not because we lack the ability to say no to temptation.

It is time for us Christians to face up to our responsibility for holiness. Too often we say we are "defeated" by this or that sin. No, we are not defeated; we are simply disobedient! It might be good if we stopped using the terms "victory" and "defeat" to describe our progress in holiness. Rather we should use the terms "obedience" and "disobedience." When I say I am defeated by some sin, I am unconsciously slipping out from under my responsibility. I am saying something outside of me has defeated me. But when I say I am disobedient, that places the responsibility for my sin squarely on me. We may, in fact, be defeated, but the reason we are defeated is because we have chosen to disobey. We have chosen to entertain lustful thoughts, or to harbor resentment, or to shade the truth a little.

We need to brace ourselves up and to realize that we are responsible for our thoughts, attitudes, and actions. We need to reckon on the fact that we died to sin's reign, that it no longer has any dominion over us, that God has united us with the risen Christ in all His power, and has given us the Holy Spirit to work in us. Only as we accept our responsibility and appropriate God's provisions will we make any progress in our pursuit of holiness.

God's Provision and Our Responsibility

(Chapters 7 and 8)

STUDY QUESTIONS

1. Carefully consider Romans 6:11. What does this verse mean to you, and how can you apply it to your life?

2. Review Isaiah 66:2 and 1 Thessalonians 5:23-24. How should we express our dependence on the Holy Spirit for holiness? What do you want to do to improve in this area?

3. From each of the following verses, write a brief statement of how the Holy Spirit helps us in our pursuit of holiness.

    •   Romans 8:9

- Romans 8:13

- Galatians 5:16

- Ephesians 3:16

- Philippians 2:12-13

4. Read the following verses, and write a statement describing your personal responsibility for holiness.

- Hebrews 12:1; James 4:7; 2 Peter 3:14

5. *(For additional study)* Look up the following verses about the Holy Spirit's work in us, write down those which are the most helpful to you, and explain why they are.

- 1 Corinthians 6:18-19; Ephesians 3:14-21; Philippians 4:11-13; Colossians 1:9-11; 1 Thessalonians 4:7-8

6. How can we express at the same time both an attitude of dependence on the Holy Spirit and acceptance of our own responsibility for holiness?

7. What application of the truths of this session do you want to make in your life?

Putting Sin to Death

Read the following portion of *The Pursuit of Holiness*. In the margins, record observations, illustrations, or questions that come to mind as you read. Then answer the study questions that follow the reading.

Chapter Nine: Putting Sin to Death

*Put to death, therefore, whatever belongs to your
earthly nature: sexual immorality, impurity,
lust, evil desires and greed, which is idolatry.*
COLOSSIANS 3:5

Notes and Observations

The New Testament leaves no doubt that holiness is our responsibility. If we are to pursue holiness, we must take some decisive action. I once discussed a particular sin problem with a person who said, "I've been praying that God would motivate me to stop." Motivate him to stop? What this person was saying in effect was that God had not done enough. It is so easy to ask God to do something more because that postpones facing up to our own responsibility.

The action we are to take is to put to death the misdeeds of the body (Romans 8:13). Paul uses the same expression in another book: "Put to death, therefore, whatever belongs to your earthly nature" (Colossians 3:5). What does the expression *put to death* mean? The *King James Version* uses the term *mortify*. According to the dictionary, mortify means "to destroy the strength, vitality, or functioning of; to subdue or deaden."[1] To put to death the misdeeds of the body, then, is to destroy the strength and vitality of sin as it tries to reign in our bodies.

It must be clear to us that mortification, though it is something we do, cannot be carried out in our own strength. Well did the Puritan John Owen say, "Mortification from a self-strength, carried on by ways of self-invention, unto the end of a self-righteousness is the soul and substance of all false religion."[2] Mortification must be done by the strength and under the direction of the Holy Spirit.

Owen says further, "The Spirit alone is sufficient for this work. All ways and means without Him are useless. He is the great efficient. He is the One who gives life and strength to our efforts."[3]

But though mortification must be done by the strength and under the direction of the Holy Spirit, it is nevertheless a work which we must do. Without the Holy Spirit's strength there will be no mortification, but without our working in His strength there will also be no mortification.

The crucial question then is, "How do we destroy the strength and vitality of sin?" If we are to work at this difficult task, we must first have *conviction*. We must be persuaded that a holy life of God's will for every Christian is important. We must believe that the pursuit of holiness is worth the effort and pain required to mortify the misdeeds of the body. We must be convinced that "without holiness no one will see the Lord" (Hebrews 12:14).

Not only must we develop conviction for living a holy life in general, but we must also develop convictions in specific areas of obedience.

These convictions are developed through exposure to the Word of God. Our minds have far too long been accustomed to the world's values. Even after we become Christians, the world around us constantly seeks to conform us to its value system. We are bombarded on every side by temptations to indulge our sinful natures. That is why Paul said, "Don't let the world around you squeeze you into its own mold, but let God remake you so that your whole attitude of mind is changed" (Romans 12:2, PH).

Only through God's Word are our minds remolded and our values renewed. When giving instructions for future kings of

Israel, God said that a copy of His Law "shall be with him, and he shall read it all the days of his life, that he may learn to fear the Lord his God, by carefully observing all the words of this law and these statutes" (Deuteronomy 17:19, NASB). The king was to read God's law all the days of his life to learn to fear the Lord. In that way he could learn the necessity of holiness, and how he might know God's specific will in various situations.

Jesus said, "Whoever has my commands and obeys them, he is the one who loves me" (John 14:21). Obedience is the pathway to holiness, but it is only as we *have* His commands that we can obey them. God's Word must be so strongly fixed in our minds that it becomes the dominant influence in our thoughts, our attitudes, and our actions. One of the most effective ways of influencing our minds is through memorizing Scripture. David said, "I have hidden your word in my heart that I might not sin against you" (Psalm 119:11).

To memorize Scripture effectively, you must have a plan. The plan should include a selection of well-chosen verses, a practical system for learning those verses, a systematic means of reviewing them to keep them fresh in your memory, and simple rules for continuing Scripture memory on your own.

I know from personal experience how important such a plan is. I instinctively realized the importance of God's Word for my life as a young Christian at college, but I did not know what to do about it. I memorized a few verses in a spasmodic and haphazard fashion, but they were of little profit to me. Then one day I was introduced to The Navigators' *Topical Memory System*, and began a plan of regular Scripture memorization. Twenty-eight years later, I still profit from this simple but effective plan for hiding God's Word in my heart.[4]

Of course, the goal of memorization is application of the Scripture to one's daily life. It is through the application of Scripture to specific life situations that we develop the kind of conviction to see us through the temptations that trip us up so easily.

A number of years ago my wife and I lived in Kansas City, Missouri, while I worked across the river in Kansas City, Kansas. As an employee working in Kansas, I was subject to Kansas state income tax, but as a resident of Missouri I did not have to pay the tax till the end of the year. We moved to Colorado in July of one year, and at the end of the year I realized that I owed Kansas for seven months of income tax. My first thought was to forget it; after all, the amount was fairly small and they wouldn't come all the way to Colorado to collect. But then the Holy Spirit brought to my mind a verse I had previously memorized, "Give everyone what you owe him: if you owe taxes, pay taxes" (Romans 13:7). God brought conviction to my heart that I must pay the State of Kansas the tax I owed out of obedience to God. God gave *conviction* that day regarding the payment of taxes, and this conviction has influenced and governed my actions ever since.

This is the way we develop conviction — by bringing God's Word to bear on specific situations that arise in our lives and determining God's will in that situation from the Word.

Many issues of life are clearly addressed in the Bible, and we would do well to memorize verses that speak to those issues. For example, God's will concerning honesty is plainly spelled out: "Therefore each of you must put off falsehood and speak truthfully to his neighbor. . . . He who has been stealing must steal no longer" (Ephesians 4:25,28). His will concerning abstinence from sexual immorality also is described clearly: "It is God's will that you should be sanctified: that you should avoid sexual immorality" (1 Thessalonians 4:3). These are clearly stated issues where we should have no difficulty developing convictions as to God's will if we are willing to obey His Word.

But what about issues that are not specifically mentioned in the Scriptures — how do we determine God's will and develop conviction in those areas?

Years ago a friend gave me what he called his "Formula:

How to Know Right from Wrong." The formula asks four questions based on three verses in 1 Corinthians:

- "'Everything is permissible for me' — but not everything is beneficial" (1 Corinthians 6:12). *Question 1:* Is it helpful — physically, spiritually, and mentally?

- "'Everything is permissible for me' — but I will not be mastered by anything" (1 Corinthians 6:12). *Question 2:* Does it bring me under its power?

- "Therefore, if what I eat causes my brother to fall into sin, I will never eat meat again, so that I will not cause him to fall" (1 Corinthians 8:13). *Question 3:* Does it hurt others?

- "So whether you eat or drink or whatever you do, do it all for the glory of God" (1 Corinthians 10:31). *Question 4:* Does it glorify God?

As simple as this formula may appear, it is powerful in developing conviction — if we are willing to use it. These questions can get rather searching. But they must be asked if we are to pursue holiness as a total way of life.

Let's apply these principles to some typical situations. Take the television programs you watch, for example. Are they helpful — physically, spiritually, or mentally? For some programs the answer may be yes, but for those to which you must honestly answer no, you should consider not viewing them.

What about the question, "Does it bring me under its power?" You may instantly apply that question to such habits as drinking, taking drugs, or smoking, and feel it doesn't apply to you. But again, what about the television set? Have certain programs "grabbed" you so that you just cannot miss them? If so,

79

they have brought you under their power. For another example, I know a Christian woman who as a teenager was a national junior tennis champion. She was so caught up in tennis that it was her whole life, even though she was a Christian. When she began to consider the claims of Christian discipleship seriously, she realized tennis held a certain power over her that was keeping her from wholly following Christ. She then made a decision to hang up her tennis racket to break that power. Not till a number of years later, when the pull was totally gone, did she begin to play tennis again solely for recreational value, and with freedom of conscience.

This illustration of the tennis player emphasizes an important fact. It may not be the activity itself that determines whether something is sinful for us, but rather our response to that activity. Certainly the game of tennis is morally neutral and, under the right conditions, physically beneficial. But because this woman had made it an idol in her life, it had become sinful for her.

Let's examine the next question, "Does it hurt others?" with this same story of my tennis-playing friend. Suppose another Christian who enjoyed playing tennis purely for recreational value had insisted to this woman that there's nothing wrong with tennis. Technically that person would be correct, but he would be insisting on a view that would likely be harmful to the young woman's spiritual life. Many activities, strictly speaking, are morally neutral, but because of some immoral associations in a person's past may be detrimental to that person, at least for a time. Those of us who do not have that immoral association must be considerate of these people lest we cause them to slip back into an activity that is sinful for them.

But what about those areas in which Christians differ in their convictions as to God's will? Paul speaks to this question in Romans 14, where he takes up the problem of eating certain food. He lays down three general principles to guide us. The first is that we should not judge those whose convictions are different from ours (verses 1-4). The second principle is that whatever our convictions are, they must be "to the Lord," that is, developed out of a sense of obedience to Him (verses 5-8). The third principle is that whatever convictions we have developed as "to the Lord," we must be true to them (verse 23). If we go against our convictions, we are sinning, even though others may have perfect freedom in that particular thing.

For several years I struggled with the question of how my family and I should observe Sunday as the Lord's Day. Early in my Christian life I was taught that Sunday was a sacred day and that its activities should be governed accordingly. I soon came to realize, however, that there is genuine disagreement among sincere Christians as to how Sunday is to be observed. Applying the principles of Romans 14 to this question, then, I must first of all not judge those who observe Sunday differently than I do. Second, whatever my own convictions, they must be out of a sincere response of obedience to how God is leading *me*. And then, having developed my own convictions, I must be careful not to violate them, regardless of what other Christians may do.

The question we must ask in a serious pursuit of holiness is this: "Am I willing to develop convictions from the Scriptures and to live by these convictions?" This is often where the rub comes. We hesitate to face up to God's standard of holiness in a specific area of life. We know that to do so will require obedience that we are unwilling to give.

This leads us to the second quality we must develop if we are to put to death the misdeeds of the body. That quality is *commitment*. Jesus said, "Any of you who does not give up everything he has cannot be my disciple" (Luke 14:33). We must honestly face the question, "Am I willing to give up a certain practice or habit that is keeping me from holiness?" It is at this point of commitment that most of us fail. We prefer to dally with sin, to try to play with it a little without getting too deeply involved.

We have the "just one more time" syndrome. We will take just one more lustful look, eat just one more rich dessert before

81

starting our diet, watch just one more television program before sitting down to our Bible study. In all of this we are postponing the day of commitment, the day when we say to sin, "Enough!"

I well recall when God spoke to me about indulging my sweet tooth. It wasn't that I was overweight; it was just that I couldn't resist any dessert that came along. I was the one who always went back for seconds at the church pie socials! Then one morning right in the middle of the Christmas festivities, when all the fudge and cookies and fruitcake were so plentiful, God spoke to my heart about this problem. My initial response was, "Lord, wait till after Christmas, and I will deal with it." I wasn't willing that day to make a commitment.

Solomon tells us that the eyes of man are never satisfied (Proverbs 27:20). One more lustful look or one more piece of pie never satisfies. In fact, quite the opposite takes place. Every time we say yes to temptation, we make it harder to say no the next time.

We must recognize that we have developed habit patterns of sin. We have developed the habit of shading the facts a little bit when it is to our advantage. We have developed the habit of giving in to the inertia that refuses to let us get up in the morning. These habits must be broken, but they never will till we make a basic commitment to a life of holiness without exceptions.

The apostle John said, "My dear children, I write this to you so that you will not sin" (1 John 2:1). The whole purpose of John's letter, he says, is that we *not* sin. One day as I was studying this chapter I realized that my personal life's objective regarding holiness was less than that of John's. He was saying, in effect, "Make it your aim *not* to sin." As I thought about this, I realized that deep within my heart my real aim was not to sin *very much.* I found it difficult to say, "Yes, Lord, from here on I will make it my aim not to sin." I realized God was calling me that day to a deeper level of commitment to holiness than I had previously been willing to make.

Can you imagine a soldier going into battle with the aim

of "not getting hit very much"? The very suggestion is ridiculous. His aim is not to get hit at all! Yet if we have not made a commitment to holiness without exception, we are like a soldier going into battle with the aim of not getting hit very much. We can be sure if that is our aim, we will be hit — not with bullets, but with temptation over and over again.

Jonathan Edwards, one of the great preachers of early American history, used to make resolutions. One of these was, "Resolved, never to do anything which I would be afraid to do if it were the last hour of my life."[5] Dare we modern-day Christians make such a resolution? Are we willing to commit ourselves to the practice of holiness without exceptions? There is no point in praying for victory over temptation if we are not willing to make a commitment to say no to it.

It is only by learning to deny temptation that we will ever put to death the misdeeds of the body. Learning this is usually a slow and painful process, fraught with much failure. Our old desires and our sinful habits are not easily dislodged. To break them requires persistence, often in the face of little success. But this is the path we must tread, painful though it may be.

Notes and Observations

Putting Sin to Death

(Chapter 9)

STUDY QUESTIONS

1. After considering Romans 8:13 and Colossians 3:5, write in your own words what it means to "put to death" the sinful deeds in our lives.

2. How do the following verses help us develop personal convictions about issues that are not specifically mentioned in the Bible?

   • 1 Corinthians 6:12-13

   • 1 Corinthians 8:4-13

   • 1 Corinthians 10:23-33

3. Read through Romans 14, and list the principles that can help us in areas in which Christians have different convictions.

4. What do the following verses teach about the importance of commitment to holiness?

   • Proverbs 27:20

   • Luke 14:33

   • 1 John 2:1

5. *(For additional study)* Consider what these verses teach about commitment, conviction, and obedience. Write down those which are the most helpful to you, and explain why they are.

   • Deuteronomy 17:18-20; Psalm 119:9-11; John 14:21; Romans 12:1-2

6. Using at least one Scripture passage to document your answer, explain how we develop conviction about the necessity of living a holy life and about obedience to God in specific areas of our lives.

7. How do you think Scripture memory can help in developing conviction?

8. What application of the truths of this session do you want to make in your life?

The Place of Personal Discipline

Read the following portion of *The Pursuit of Holiness*. In the margins, record observations, illustrations, or questions that come to mind as you read. Then answer the study questions that follow the reading.

Chapter Ten: The Place of Personal Discipline

Have nothing to do with godless myths and old wives'
tales; rather, train yourself to be godly.
1 TIMOTHY 4:7

It is possible to establish convictions regarding a life of holiness, and even make a definite commitment to that end, yet fail to achieve the goal. Life is strewn with broken resolutions. We may determine by God's grace to stop a particular sinful habit—entertaining lustful thoughts, criticizing our Christian brother, or whatever. But alas, only too frequently we find we don't succeed. We do not achieve that progress in holiness we so intensely desire.

Jay Adams puts his finger on the problem when he says, "You may have sought and tried to obtain *instant* godliness. There is no such thing. . . . We want somebody to give us three easy steps to godliness, and we'll take them next Friday and be godly. The trouble is, godliness doesn't come that way."[1]

Adams goes on to show that the way to obtain godliness is through Christian discipline.[2] But the concept of discipline is suspect in our society today. It appears counter to our emphasis on freedom in Christ and often smacks of legalism and harshness.

Yet Paul says we are to train or discipline ourselves to be godly (1 Timothy 4:7). The figure of speech he uses comes from the physical training that Greek athletes went through. Paul also said, "Everyone who competes in the games goes into strict training" (I Corinthians 9:25). He said this was an attitude of his life, and one that each Christian should have (I Corinthians 9:24-27). If an athlete disciplines himself to obtain a temporal prize, he said, how much more should we Christians discipline ourselves to obtain a crown that lasts forever.

As these verses indicate, discipline is structured training. *Webster's New Collegiate Dictionary* lists as one definition of discipline, "training that corrects, molds, or perfects the mental faculties or moral character."[3] This is what we must do if we pursue holiness: We must correct, mold, and train our moral character.

Discipline toward holiness begins with the Word of God. Paul said, "All Scripture is God-breathed and is useful for teaching, rebuking, correcting and training in righteousness" (2 Timothy 3:16). The last item he mentions is *training* or *discipline* in doing righteousness. This is what the Scriptures will do for us if we use them. Jay Adams says, "It is by willing, prayerful and persistent obedience to the requirements of the Scriptures that godly patterns are developed and come to be a part of us."[4]

We read in Scripture, "You were taught . . . to put off your old self . . . to be made new in the attitude of your minds; and to put on the new self, created to be like God in true righteousness and holiness" (Ephesians 4:22-24). Where are we taught these things? Only in the Word of God. Discipline toward holiness begins then with the Scriptures — with a disciplined plan for regular intake of the Scriptures and a disciplined plan for applying them to our daily lives.

Here our cooperation with the Holy Spirit is very clear. A diagram of our interaction with the Spirit looks like this:

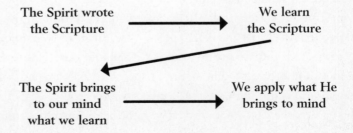

The Spirit wrote the Scripture → We learn the Scripture

The Spirit brings to our mind what we learn → We apply what He brings to mind

The Holy Spirit has already done a good part of His work by providing us with the Scriptures to discipline us. And as we learn them, He will faithfully bring them to our minds as we need them to face temptations. As we seek to apply His Word to daily situations, He will work in us to strengthen us. But we must respond to what the Holy Spirit has already done if we are to expect Him to do more.

So we see that we must discipline our lives for a regular healthy diet of the Word of God. We need a planned time each day for reading or studying the Bible. Every Christian who makes progress in holiness is a person who has disciplined his life so that he spends regular time in the Bible. There simply is no other way.

Satan will always battle us at this point. He will try to persuade us that we are too sleepy in the morning, too busy during the day, and too tired at night. It seems there is never a suitable time for the Word of God. This means we must discipline ourselves to provide this time in our daily schedules. I have found the early morning hour before breakfast to be the most profitable time for me to read the Bible and pray over areas of concern and need. That is also the only time of day when I can be consistent in my principal means of exercise — jogging. To do all this before breakfast requires that I get up at five o'clock. And since I need about seven hours of sleep each night, that means I must be in bed — lights out — by ten p.m. That is hard to do. It can only be done by disciplining my evening hours.

Some wives may not find this time before breakfast practical, especially if they have very young children or must get the rest of the family off to work or school at an early hour. In this case they may find the time immediately after breakfast to be most suitable for time alone with God. This, too, requires discipline to take time when the responsibilities of the day are demanding attention.

Whether before breakfast or after, morning or evening, the point is we must all arrange our schedules to provide for this daily intake of the Word of God.

A disciplined intake of the Word of God not only involves a planned *time*; it also involves a planned *method*. Usually we think of methods of intake as falling into four categories — *hearing* the Word taught by our pastors and teachers (Jeremiah 3:15), *reading* the Bible ourselves (Deuteronomy 17:19), *studying* the Scriptures intently (Proverbs 2:1-5), and *memorizing* key passages (Psalm 119:11). All of these methods are needed for a balanced intake of the Word. Pastors are gifted by God and trained to teach the "whole counsel of God." Reading the Scripture gives us the overall perspective of divine truth, while study of a passage or topic enables us to dig more deeply into a particular truth. Memorization helps us retain important truths so we can apply them in our lives.

But if we are to pursue holiness with discipline, we must do more than hear, read, study, or memorize Scripture. We must meditate on it. God said to Joshua, as he was assuming leadership over Israel, "Do not let this Book of the Law depart from your mouth; meditate on it day and night, so that you may be careful to do everything written in it" (Joshua 1:8). To meditate on the Scriptures is to think about them, turning them over in our minds, and applying them to our life's situations. Few of us practice meditation on the Scriptures. Somehow the idea of meditation sounds like something medieval monks did in monasteries. Yet Joshua, a very busy commander-in-chief of the army of Israel, was told to meditate on the law of God day and night.

The practice of meditation on the Word of God — simply thinking about it and its application to life — is a practice we develop through discipline. Most of us think we don't have time for this, but there are blocks of minutes during the day when we can meditate if we develop the habit.

I am something of a "bug" for the daily news and I enjoy listening to the news on the radio as I drive to and from work or elsewhere. One day I was challenged by the example of a friend to use that time to meditate on Scripture verses. Now I am surprised at how many minutes I can use to think about

Scripture passages and their application to my life. You may not have the same opportunity I have to meditate as you drive, but if you prayerfully think about it, you will probably find other opportunities in your schedule.[5]

The objective of our meditation is application — obedience to the Scriptures. This too requires discipline. Obeying the Scriptures usually requires change in our patterns of life. Because we are sinful by nature, we have developed sinful patterns, which we call habits. Discipline is required to break any habit. If a boy has developed the wrong style of swinging a baseball bat, he cannot just decide to change instantly. He has developed a certain habit, and much discipline — much correction and training — is required to break that bad habit and develop a new one.

In the same way, our patterns of disobedience to God have been developed over a number of years and are not broken easily or without discipline. Discipline does not mean gritting your teeth and saying, "I'll not do that anymore." Rather, discipline means structured, planned training. Just as you need a plan for regular Bible reading or study, so you need a plan for applying the Word to your life.

As you read or study the Scriptures and meditate on them during the day, ask yourself these three questions:

1. What does this passage teach concerning God's will for a holy life?
2. How does my life measure up to that Scripture; specifically where and how do I fall short? (Be specific; don't generalize.)
3. What definite steps of action do I need to take to obey?

The most important part of this process is the specific application of the Scripture to specific life situations. We are prone to vagueness at this point because commitment to specific actions makes us uncomfortable. But we must avoid general commit-ments to obedience and instead aim for specific obedience in specific instances. We deceive our souls when we grow in know-ledge of the truth without specifically responding to it (James 1:22). This may lead to spiritual pride (1 Corinthians 8:1).

Suppose you were meditating on 1 Corinthians 13, the great love chapter. As you think about the chapter, you realize the importance of love, and you also see the practical outworkings of love: Love is patient and kind and does not envy. You ask your-self, "Am I impatient or unkind or envious toward anyone?" As you think about this, you realize you are envious toward Joe at work who seems to be getting all the breaks. You confess this sin to God, being very specific to name Joe and your sinful reaction to his good fortune. You ask God to bless him even more and to give you a spirit of contentment so that you will not continue to envy Joe, but will instead love him. You might memorize 1 Corinthians 13:4 and think about it as you see Joe at work. You even look for ways to help him. Then you do the same thing tomorrow and the next day and the next till finally you see God working a spirit of love in your heart toward Joe.

This is discipline toward holiness. You will never put to death that spirit of envy toward Joe without a definitely struc-tured plan for doing it. That plan is what we call discipline.

You can readily see that this structured training in holiness is a lifelong process. So a necessary ingredient of discipline is *perseverance*.

Any training — physical, mental, or spiritual — is character-ized at first by failure. We fail more often than we succeed. But if we persevere, we gradually see progress till we are succeeding more often than failing. This is true as we seek to put to death particular sins. At first it seems we are making no progress, so we become discouraged and think, *What's the use? I can never over-come that sin.* That is exactly what Satan wants us to think.

It is at this point that we must exercise perseverance. We keep wanting instant success, but holiness doesn't come that way. Our sinful habits are not broken overnight. Follow-through is required to make any change in our lives, and follow-through requires perseverance.

Jonathan Edwards, who resolved never to do anything he would be afraid to do if it were the last hour of his life, also made this resolution: "Resolved, never to give over, nor in the least to slacken, my fight with my corruptions, however unsuccessful I may be."[6] At first glance these two resolutions seem somewhat contradictory. If Edwards had resolved never to do anything he shouldn't do, then why talk about never giving up the fight regardless of how *unsuccessful* he might be? Was he not sincere in making the first resolution? Yes, he was sincere, but he also knew there would be much failure and that perseverance was required. So he first resolved to seek to live a holy life, then to persevere despite the failures he knew would come.

A verse of Scripture I often use in the face of failure with my own sins is Proverbs 24:16: "For though a righteous man falls seven times, he rises again, but the wicked are brought down by calamity." The person who is disciplining himself toward holiness falls many times, but he doesn't quit. After each failure he gets up and continues the struggle. Not so with the unrighteous. He stumbles in his sin and gives up. He has no power to overcome because he does not have the Spirit of God at work in him.

One of the chapters in the Bible we have the most trouble with is Romans 7. Christians are always trying to "get out of Romans 7 and into Romans 8." The reason we don't like Romans 7 is because it so accurately mirrors our own struggle with sin. And we don't like the idea that we have to struggle with sin. We want instant victory. We want to "walk in the Spirit and let Him win the victory." But God wants us to persevere in discipline toward holiness.

Some feel that such statements of Paul's as "For what I want to do I do not do, but what I hate I do" (Romans 7:15) are too strong for a Christian walking in the Spirit. But what Christian can deny that this is often his own experience? The truth is, the more we see the holiness of God and His law revealed to us in the Scripture, the more we recognize how far short we fall.

Isaiah was a prophet of God, walking in the righteousness of God's commandments. Yet on seeing the Lord God in His holiness, he was compelled to cry out, "Woe is me! . . . I am ruined! For I am a man of unclean lips, and I live among a people of unclean lips, and my eyes have seen the King, the Lord Almighty" (Isaiah 6:5).

As we grow in the *knowledge* of God's holiness, even though we are also growing in the *practice* of holiness it seems the gap between our knowledge and our practice always gets wider. This is the Holy Spirit's way of drawing us to more and more holiness. This is illustrated by the following graph:

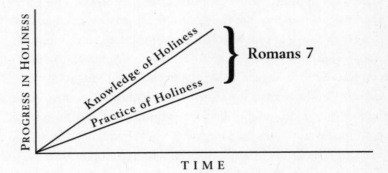

As we progress in holiness, we come to hate sin (Psalm 119:104) and to delight in God's law (Romans 7:22). We see the perfection of God's law and the rightness of all He requires of us. We agree that "his commands are not burdensome" (1 John 5:3), but are "holy, righteous, and good" (Romans 7:12). But during all this time we also see our own inner corruption and our frequent falls into sin. We cry out with Paul, "What a wretched man I am!" (Romans 7:24), and we want to give up. This we dare not do. If we would succeed in our pursuit of holiness we must persevere in spite of failure.

The Place of Personal Discipline

(Chapter 10)

STUDY QUESTIONS

1. What does each of the following passages teach about Christian discipline?

    *   1 Corinthians 9:24-27

    *   1 Timothy 4:7-8

    *   2 Timothy 3:16

2. Look up the following verses. Why is perseverance needed in Christian discipline? How can these verses help us to persevere?

    *   Proverbs 24:16; 1 Corinthians 15:58; Hebrews 12:3

3. *(For additional study)* Examine how each of these verses relates to discipline in the Christian life. Write down those which are the most helpful to you, and explain why they are.

    •   Joshua 1:8-9; Romans 7:15; Ephesians 4:20-24; Hebrews 12:1-2; James 1:22-25

4. What does it mean to meditate on Scripture? Suggest a plan for meditation that would be suitable for you and your schedule.

5. In your own words, write a definition of discipline.

6. What application of the truths of this session do you want to make in your life?

Holiness in Body

Read the following portion of *The Pursuit of Holiness*. In the margins, record observations, illustrations, or questions that come to mind as you read. Then answer the study questions that follow the reading.

Chapter Eleven: Holiness in Body

No, I beat my body and make it my slave so that after I have preached to others, I myself will not be disqualified for the prize.
1 CORINTHIANS 9:27

True holiness includes control over our physical bodies and appetites. If we are to pursue holiness we must recognize that our bodies are temples of the Holy Spirit and that we are to glorify God with them.

Modern Christians, especially those in the Western world, have generally been found wanting in the area of holiness of body. Gluttony and laziness, for example, were regarded by earlier Christians as sin. Today we may look on these as weaknesses of the will but certainly not sin. We even joke about our overeating and other indulgences instead of crying out to God in confession and repentance.

Our physical bodies and natural appetites were created by God and are not sinful in themselves. Nevertheless, if left uncontrolled, we will find our bodies becoming "instruments of wickedness" rather than "instruments of righteousness" (Romans 6:13). We will be pursuing the "cravings of sinful man" (1 John 2:16) instead of holiness. If we watch ourselves closely, we can see how often we eat and drink just to gratify physical desire; how often we lie in bed in the morning simply because we don't "feel" like getting up when we should; how often we give in to immoral looks and thoughts simply to satisfy the sin-tainted sex drive within us.

Michel Quoist, in his book *The Christian Response*, says, "If your body makes all the decisions and gives all the orders, and if you obey, the physical can effectively destroy every other dimension of your personality. Your emotional life will be blunted and your spiritual life will be stifled and ultimately will become anemic."[1] Over 200 years ago Susannah Wesley wrote, "Whatever increases the strength and authority of your body over your mind — that thing is sin to you."[2]

The apostle Paul emphasized the need to keep our natural appetites and desires under control. He spoke of his body as his adversary, as the instrument through which appetites and lusts, if left unchecked, would war against his soul (1 Corinthians 9:27). He was determined that his body with these appetites would be his slave, not his master.

Paul further urged us to present our bodies a living and holy sacrifice, acceptable to God, and to not be conformed to this world (Romans 12:1-2). Quite possibly there is no greater conformity to the world among evangelical Christians today than the way in which we, instead of presenting our bodies as holy sacrifices, pamper and indulge them in defiance of our better judgment and our Christian purpose in life.

I am not here singling out those who have a so-called "weight problem." Those of us who can eat what we please without gaining weight may be more guilty of gluttony and indulging the appetites of the body than the person who struggles — often with failure — to control his appetite for food. On the other hand, the overweight person should not excuse his failure. We should all examine ourselves as to whether we eat and drink to the glory of God, recognizing that our bodies are the temples of the Holy Spirit.

The Mormon people are noted for their abstinence from tobacco, liquor, and all beverages containing caffeine. We Christians may shrug off their abstinence as legalistic and as one more group's list of prohibitions. But we should not miss the point that their actions are a practical response to their belief that their bodies are the temple of God. For the Christian, his body truly is the temple of God. How sad, then, that a false religion should be more diligent in this area than we Christians. Let me be emphatic: I am neither approving nor disapproving the Mormons' particular list of prohibitions. But we need to ask ourselves if our consumption of food and drink is controlled by an awareness that our bodies are the temples of the Holy Spirit.

Another reason we must closely govern our indulgence of food and drink is that the person who overindulges his body at this point will find it more and more difficult to mortify other sinful deeds of the body. The habit of always giving in to the desire for food or drink will extend to other areas. If we cannot say no to an indulgent appetite, we will be hard pressed to say no to lustful thoughts. There must be an attitude of diligent obedience in every area if we are to succeed in mortifying any one expression of sin. Thomas Boston wrote, "They that would keep themselves pure must have their bodies in subjection, and that may require, in some cases, a holy violence."[3]

Along with such sins of the body as sexual immorality, impurity, lust, and evil desires, Paul also mentions greed, which he says is idolatry (Colossians 3:5). While greed often manifests itself in its basic form — the sheer love of money for money's sake — it more often is seen in what we call materialism. Not many of us want to be extremely rich; we just want all the nice things the world around us considers important.

Materialism wars against our souls in a twofold manner. First, it makes us discontent and envious of others. Second, it leads us to pamper and indulge our bodies so that we become soft and lazy. As we become soft and lazy in our bodies, we tend to become soft and lazy spiritually. When Paul talked about making his body his slave, so that after having preached to others he himself would not be disqualified, he was not thinking about physical disqualification, but spiritual.

99

He knew well that physical softness inevitably leads to spiritual softness. When the body is pampered and indulged, the instincts and passions of the body tend to get the upper hand and dominate our thoughts and actions. We tend to do not what we *should* do, but what we *want* to do, as we follow the cravings of our sinful nature.

There is no place for laziness and indulgence of the body in a disciplined pursuit of holiness. We have to learn to say no to the body instead of continually giving in to its momentary desires. We tend to act according to our feelings. The trouble is, we seldom "feel" like doing what we should do. We don't feel like getting out of bed to have our morning time with God, or doing Bible study, or praying, or anything else we should do. That is why we have to take control of our bodies and make them our servants instead of our masters.

The place to start controlling the cravings of our physical appetites is to reduce our exposure to temptation. Our sinful cravings are strengthened by temptation. When a suitable temptation is presented to us, our cravings seem to get new vigor and power. Paul had definite words of instruction for us on this subject. He told us, "Flee the evil desires of youth" (2 Timothy 2:22). Some temptations can best be overcome by fleeing. He also said, "Do not think about how to gratify the desires of your sinful nature" (Romans 13:14). Do not plan ahead or make provision for ways to indulge your bodily appetites.

Several years ago I realized I had developed a craving for ice cream. Now there is nothing wrong with ice cream in itself; it was just that I had indulged myself so much that it had become a craving. When I shared this problem with my wife, she stopped keeping ice cream in the freezer. She helped me stop making provision to fulfill that particular desire, which, through overindulgence, had become sin for me. Several years ago I also canceled my subscription to a popular magazine because I noticed many of the articles tended to stimulate impure thoughts in my mind.

We are to flee temptation and take positive steps to avoid it, and we are to avoid thinking how to gratify our sinful desires. "The prudent see danger and take refuge, but the simple keep going and suffer for it" (Proverbs 27:12).

We should also study our sinful desires and how they rise up against us. John Owen said, "To labor to be acquainted with the ways, wiles, methods, advantages, and occasions of the success of sin, is the beginning to this warfare."[4] Consider beforehand. It is amazing how often we walk into known areas of temptation without any plan or resolution as to how we will react. If you have a weakness for sweets as I have, and you must go to the church pie social, plan beforehand what you will do. A number of years ago, a friend who was a new Christian was invited to a roller skating party with a Christian youth group. He decided not to go because, before becoming a Christian, he had frequently made "pick-ups" at roller rinks. He felt that at that time in his growth, to return to that environment would tend to stimulate his old lustful desires. So he decided to "flee," to "make no provision for the flesh." He was able to do this because he considered beforehand the possible consequences of going to a seemingly innocent roller skating party.

God expects us to assume our responsibilities for keeping the sinful desires of the body under control. It is true we cannot do this in our own strength. Our sinful desires, stimulated by all the temptations around us, are too strong for us. But though we cannot do it by ourselves, we can do it. As we set ourselves to the task in dependence upon the Holy Spirit, we will see Him at work in us. We will fail many times, but as we persevere, we will be able to say with Paul, "I can do everything through him who gives me strength" (Philippians 4:13).

Holiness in Body

(Chapter 11)

STUDY QUESTIONS

1. The following three verses give practical ways to resist temptation. In what areas of your life can these verses help you?

    •   Proverbs 27:12

    •   Romans 13:14

    •   2 Timothy 2:22

2. *(For additional study)* Examine how each of these verses relates to bodily holiness. Write down those which are the most helpful to you, and explain why they are.

    • Philippians 3:17-19; Colossians 3:5-7; 1 Timothy 6:17; Hebrews 13:5; 1 John 2:15-16

3. After reading the following verses, write a statement about the importance of holiness in body.

    • Romans 6:12-13; 12:1-2; 1 Corinthians 6:19-20; 9:27

4. Why is it important for the Christian to govern his indulgence of food and drink?

5. In what ways does materialism affect our holiness of body?

6.   What application of the truths of this session do you want to make in your life?

Holiness in Spirit

Read the following portion of *The Pursuit of Holiness*. In the margins, record observations, illustrations, or questions that come to mind as you read. Then answer the study questions that follow the reading.

Chapter Twelve: Holiness in Spirit

Since we have these promises, dear friends, let us purify ourselves
from everything that contaminates body and spirit, perfecting
holiness out of reverence for God.
2 CORINTHIANS 7:1

A number of years ago in campus evangelism, we used an illustration calculated to make our collegiate audiences vividly aware that they were personally sinners. We would say, "If I could flash on a screen before us tonight all of your thoughts of this past week, you would have to leave town." This remark not only made the point, but always drew a laugh. But for the Christian, such a charge is no laughing matter. Our thoughts are just as important to God as our actions, and are known to God as clearly as our actions (Psalm 139:1-4; 1 Samuel 16:7).

Jesus taught us in the Sermon on the Mount that God's commands are intended not only to regulate outward conduct, but inner disposition as well. It is not enough that we do not kill; we must also not hate. It is not enough that we do not commit adultery; we must not even entertain lustful looks and thoughts.

Just as we must learn to bring the appetites of our bodies under control, so we must also learn to bring our thought lives under obedience to Jesus Christ. In fact, Paul warns us against misguided and wrongly motivated attempts to control the body that leave our thought lives unrestrained (Colossians 2:23). It is

105

possible to curb the natural appetites of the body outwardly and yet be filled with all manner of inner defilement.

The Bible indicates that our thought lives ultimately determine our character. Solomon said, "For as he thinks within himself, so he is" (Proverbs 23:7, NASB). An old well-known verse puts it this way:

Sow a thought, reap an act;
Sow an act, reap a habit;
Sow a habit, reap a character.

It is because of the importance of our thought lives that Paul said, "Finally, brothers, whatever is true, whatever is noble, whatever is right, whatever is pure, whatever is lovely, whatever is admirable — if anything is excellent or praiseworthy — think about such things" (Philippians 4:8).

As Christians we are no longer to be conformed to the pattern of this world but we are to be renewed in our minds (Romans 12:1-2; Ephesians 4:23; 1 Peter 1:14). Holiness begins in our minds and works out to our actions. This being true, what we allow to enter our minds is critically important.

The television programs we watch, the movies we may attend, the books and magazines we read, the music we listen to, and the conversations we have all affect our minds. We need to evaluate the effects of these avenues honestly, using Philippians 4:8 as a standard. Are the thoughts stimulated by these various avenues true? Are they pure, lovely, admirable, excellent, or praiseworthy?

The world around us constantly seeks to conform our minds to its sinful ways. It is earnest and pressing in its endeavors. It will entice and persuade us (Proverbs 1:10-14). When we resist, it will ridicule and abuse us as "old-fashioned" and "puritanical" (1 Peter 4:4).

Too many Christians, instead of resisting, are more and more giving ground to the world's constant pressure. A few years ago sincere Christians were quite selective about the movies they attended, if they attended them at all. Today the same movies that were avoided are being shown on television in the living rooms of Christians across the nation. A friend of mine told me of a young couple in full-time Christian work who came to him wanting to know if it was wrong to attend X-rated movies! That the question should even be entertained illustrates the degree to which the world has infected our minds.

The music we listen to often carries the message of the world, and the world uses the medium of music to squeeze us into its mold. And a Christian cannot help being gradually influenced if he continually listens to the world's music.

Perhaps it should go without saying that Christians are to abstain from indulging in or listening to suggestive stories and jokes. But Paul could not take this for granted among the early churches, and neither can we in this century. Listen to Paul's clear warning on the subject: "But among you there must not be even a hint of sexual immorality, or of any kind of impurity, or of greed, because these are improper for God's holy people. Nor should there be obscenity, foolish talk or coarse joking, which are out of place, but rather thanksgiving" (Ephesians 5:3-4). "Not even a hint of immorality" places any suggestive speech whatsoever outside the bounds of a holy walk.

Another stimulus to impure thoughts we must be alert for is what our eyes see. Jesus warned against the lustful look (Matthew 5:28). Job made a covenant with his eyes (Job 31:1). David's wanton look was almost fatal to his spiritual life (2 Samuel 11:2). Not only must we guard our own eyes; we must be careful that we are not the source of temptation to others. For this reason, modesty of dress and actions is required among both men and women (1 Timothy 2:9; 5:2).

But Philippians 4:8 speaks to more than just immoral and unclean thoughts. Our thoughts must not only be pure — they must also be true, lovely, and praiseworthy. Just as we can commit adultery in our hearts (Matthew 5:28), so we can also commit murder in our hearts (Matthew 5:21-22).

In one of his letters, Paul listed some acts of the sinful nature. These included defilements of the body — sexual immorality, impurity, debauchery, drunkenness, orgies, and the like. Others in the list defile the spirit: hatred, discord, jealousy, fits of rage, selfish ambition, and so on. We must purify ourselves not only from the gross sins of the body, but also from the more "acceptable" sins of the spirit.

Alas, here again we Christians have so often failed miserably. Focusing on our particular group's list of do's and don'ts, we neglect the inner life where envy, pride, bitterness, and a critical, unforgiving spirit may reign unchecked.

The elder brother in the story of the prodigal son (Luke 15) is a classic example of one who led an exemplary outward life but who was consumed by a spirit of envy and self-righteousness. He could claim never to have disobeyed his father's commandments, yet his jealousy and anger over his father's joy in the return of his prodigal brother marks him to this day as an example to be shunned rather than followed.

The spirit of envy was the root of King Saul's unrelenting warfare against David. Initially Saul was highly pleased with David and set him over his men of war. But one day Saul heard the women of Israel singing, "Saul has slain his thousands, and David his tens of thousands" (1 Samuel 18:7). Saul was very angry that they had ascribed ten thousand to David and to him only thousands. And the Scripture says, "Saul looked at David with suspicion from that day on" (1 Samuel 18:9, NASB). God has placed each one of us in the body of Christ as it has pleased Him (1 Corinthians 12:18), and has assigned to each of us a place in life (1 Corinthians 7:17). To some God has assigned a place of prominence, to others a place of obscurity; to some a place of wealth, to others a place of daily struggle to make ends meet. But regardless of our station in life or place in the Body, there is always the temptation to envy someone else. The elder brother would one day inherit all his father's possessions, yet he became jealous over a banquet to celebrate his brother's return. Saul was king over all Israel but could not stand someone else receiving more praise than he.

The cure for the sin of envy and jealousy is to find our contentment in God. Asaph in Psalm 73 was envious of the wicked as he saw their apparent prosperity (verse 3). He felt his pursuit of a holy life was in vain (verse 13). Only when he was enabled to say to God, "Earth has nothing I desire besides you" (verse 25), was he delivered from the sin of envy.

Another defilement of spirit that has shipwrecked many Christians is *bitterness*. Bitterness arises in our hearts when we do not trust in the sovereign rule of God in our lives. If ever anyone had a reason to be bitter it was Joseph. Sold by his jealous brothers into slavery, falsely accused by his master's immoral wife, and forgotten by one he had helped in prison, Joseph never lost sight of the fact that God was in control of all that happened to him. In the end he was able to say to his brothers, "You intended to harm me, but God intended it for good to accomplish what is now being done, the saving of many lives" (Genesis 50:20).

We can become bitter against God or against other people. Asaph was bitter against God because he felt God was not giving him a fair shake in life (Psalm 73:21). Job was bitter because he felt God was not recognizing his righteousness and even came to the place where his attitude was described as, "It profits a man nothing when he tries to please God" (Job 34:9).

Bitterness toward people is the result of an *unforgiving spirit*. Someone has wronged us, either apparently or actually, and we refuse to forgive that person. Instead we harbor thoughts of bitterness toward the person. We refuse to forgive because we will not recognize that God has forgiven us of far, far greater wrongs. We are like the servant who, having just been forgiven a debt of several million dollars, had a fellow servant thrown into prison over a debt of a few dollars (Matthew 18:21-35).

Closely akin to bitterness is the *spirit of retaliation*. When we are wronged, the tendency is to retaliate — often in our minds if not in actions. When David was fleeing the insurrection of his son Absalom in Jerusalem, Shimei of the family of Saul came out to curse David and throw stones at him. One of David's men wanted to retaliate by killing Shimei, but David restrained him with these words: "Leave him alone; let him curse, for the Lord has told him to. It may be that the Lord will see my distress and repay me with good for the cursing I am receiving today" (2 Samuel 16:11-12).

Paul wrote, "Do not take revenge, my friends, but leave room for God's wrath, for it is written: 'It is mine to avenge, I will repay,' says the Lord" (Romans 12:19). Peter said of our Lord, "When they hurled their insults at him, he did not retaliate; when he suffered, he made no threats. Instead, he entrusted himself to him who judges justly" (1 Peter 2:23). This is the way to cleanse ourselves from the defiling spirit of retaliation: to entrust ourselves to Him who judges justly and who said, "It is Mine to avenge, I will repay."

One of the most difficult defilements of spirit to deal with is the *critical spirit*. A critical spirit has its root in pride. Because of the "plank" of pride in our own eye we are not capable of dealing with the "speck" of need in someone else. We are often like the Pharisee who, completely unconscious of his own need, prayed, "God, I thank you that I am not like other men" (Luke 18:11). We are quick to see — and to speak of — the faults of others, but slow to see our own needs. How sweetly we relish the opportunity to speak critically of someone else — even when we are unsure of our facts. We forget that "a man who stirs up dissension among brothers" by criticizing one to another is one of the "six things which the Lord hates" (Proverbs 6:16-19).

All of these attitudes — envy, jealousy, bitterness, an unforgiving and retaliatory spirit, and a critical and gossiping spirit — defile us and keep us from being holy before God. They are just as evil as immorality, drunkenness, and debauchery. Therefore, we must work diligently at rooting out these sinful attitudes from our minds. Often we are not even aware our attitudes are sinful. We cloak these defiling thoughts under the guise of justice and righteous indignation. But we need to pray daily for humility and honesty to see these sinful attitudes for what they really are, and then for grace and discipline to root them out of our minds and replace them with thoughts pleasing to God.

Notes and Observations

Holiness in Spirit

(Chapter 12)

STUDY QUESTIONS

1. From each of the following verses, write a statement about the importance of holiness in our thoughts.

    •   1 Samuel 16:7

    •   Psalm 139:1-4

    •   2 Corinthians 7:1

2. Compare your own thought life with the standard set for us in Philippians 4:8. What types of thoughts do you need to avoid? What types of thoughts do you want to cultivate?

3. How we think is affected by what we see and hear. From the following verses, explain the Bible's standards in these two areas.

    •   Matthew 5:27-28; Ephesians 5:3-4; 1 Timothy 2:9-10

4. Study Galatians 5:19-21. Which of these acts of the sinful nature listed in the passage are most apt to be present in Christians? Which do you think are the most dangerous to you in your life?

5. Describe the unholy thinking referred to in each of the following passages.

    •   1 Samuel 18:6-12

    •   Psalm 73:12-14,21

    •   Matthew 18:21-35

- Luke 15:22-32

- Luke 18:9-14

6. *(For additional study)* Examine how each of the following verses relates to holiness in spirit, write down those which are the most helpful to you, and explain why they are.

   - Genesis 37:3-11; Job 31:1; Proverbs 1:10-16; Matthew 5:21-22; Romans 12:19; 1 Peter 2:21-23; 4:3-5

7. What application of the truths of this session do you want to make in your life?

Holiness and Our Wills

Read the following portion of *The Pursuit of Holiness*. In the margins, record observations, illustrations, or questions that come to mind as you read. Then answer the study questions that follow the reading.

Chapter Thirteen: Holiness and Our Wills

For it is God who works in you to will and
to act according to his good purpose.
PHILIPPIANS 2:13

Notes and Observations

In all that has been said so far about our responsibility for holiness — the necessity of conviction and commitment, perseverance and discipline, and of holiness in body and in spirit — the activity of our wills is always implied. It is the will that ultimately makes each individual choice of whether we will sin or obey. It is the will that chooses to yield to temptation or to say no. Our wills, then, ultimately determine our moral destiny, whether we will be holy or unholy in our character and conduct.

This being true, it is critically important that we understand how our wills function — what causes them to turn in one direction or the other, why they make the choices they do. Above all else, we must learn how to bring our wills into submission and obedience to the will of God on a practical, daily, hour-by-hour basis.

To help us understand how our wills function, let us review the definition of the heart presented earlier in session 4 (chapter 6). In that definition Owen said the heart as used in the Bible generally denotes all the faculties of the soul as they work together in doing good or evil — the mind, the emotions, the conscience, and the will.

These faculties were all implanted in man's soul by God, but were all corrupted through man's fall in the Garden of Eden. Our reason (or understanding) was darkened (Ephesians 4:18), our desires were entangled (Ephesians 2:3), and our wills perverted (John 5:40). With new birth our reason is again enlightened, our affections and desires redirected, and our wills subdued. But though this is true, it is not true all at once. In actual experience it is a growing process. We are told to renew our minds (Romans 12:2), to set our affections on things above (Colossians 3:1),[1] and to submit our wills to God (James 4:7).

Moreover, when God originally created man, the reason, the emotions, and the will all worked in perfect harmony. Reason led the way in understanding the will of God, the will consented to God's will, and the emotions delighted in doing it. But with the entrance of sin into man's soul, these three faculties began to work at cross-purposes to one another and to God. The will has become stubborn and rebellious and will not consent to that which reason knows to be the will of God. Or, more commonly, the emotions get the upper hand and draw away both reason and will from obedience to God.

The point of all this is to emphasize and enable us to understand the interrelation of the mind, emotions, and will. While the will is the ultimate determiner of all choices, it is influenced in its choices by the strongest forces brought to bear upon it.

These compelling forces come from a variety of sources. It may be the subtle suggestions of Satan and his world system (Ephesians 2:2) or the evil enticements of our own sinful nature (James 1:14). It may be the urgent voice of conscience, the earnest reasoning of a loving friend, or the quiet prompting of the Holy Spirit. But from whatever source these compelling forces come, they reach our wills through either our reason or our emotions.

Therefore we must guard what enters our minds and what influences our emotions. Solomon said, "Watch over your heart with all diligence, for from it flow the springs of life" (Proverbs

4:23, NASB). If we diligently guard our minds and emotions, we will see the Holy Spirit working in us to conform our wills to His own (Philippians 2:12-13). How then do we guard our minds and emotions?

David said, "How can a young man keep his way pure? By living according to your word" (Psalm 119:9). David guarded his way with the Word of God. The Bible speaks to us primarily through our reason, and this is why it is so vitally important for our minds to be constantly brought under its influence. There is absolutely no shortcut to holiness that bypasses or gives little priority to a consistent intake of the Bible.

Solomon told us that wisdom, understanding, and discretion will guard us from the evil way (Proverbs 2:10-12). These are qualities of our minds. How do we acquire these qualities? "For the Lord gives wisdom; from his mouth come knowledge and understanding" (Proverbs 2:6). But to whom does the Lord give these qualities? He gives them to the one who receives His sayings, who inwardly treasures His commandments, who makes his ear alert to wisdom and his heart ready for understanding, who prays for discernment and understanding, and who seeks understanding as if it were hidden treasure (Proverbs 2:1-5).

It is obvious from even a casual reading of Proverbs 2:1-12 that the protective influence of the Word of God comes as a result of diligent, prayerful, and purposeful intake of Scripture. To guard our minds, we must give priority to the Bible in our lives — not just for the spiritual information it gives but also for the daily application of it in our workaday lives.

Not only must we guard our minds, we must also guard our emotions. To do this, it is helpful first to realize that while God most often appeals to our wills through our reason, sin and Satan usually appeal to us through our desires. It is true Satan will attack our reason to confuse and cloud the issues, but that is only to enable him to conquer us through our desires. This is the strategy he employed with Eve (Genesis 3:1-6). He attacked her reason by questioning God's integrity, but his primary temptation was to her desire. We read that Eve saw that the tree was *good* for food, it was a *delight* to the eyes, and *desirable* for making one wise (Genesis 3:6).

Knowing that Satan attacks primarily through our desires, we should watch over them diligently and bring the Word of God to bear on them constantly. This is not asceticism; it is spiritual prudence. Each of us should seek to be aware of how sin attacks us through our desires and take preventive actions. This is what Paul urged Timothy to do when he instructed him to "flee the evil desires of youth" (2 Timothy 2:22).

But the guarding of our desires is more than fighting a rearguard defensive action against temptations from the world, the flesh, and the devil. We must take the offensive. Paul directs us to set our hearts on things above, that is, on spiritual values (Colossians 3:1). The psalmist encourages us to *delight* ourselves in the law of God (Psalm 1:2), and it was said prophetically of Jesus, "I *delight* to do Thy will, O my God" (Psalm 40:8, NASB, emphasis added). So we see that we are to set our desires on spiritual things and delight ourselves in the law and will of God.

So we have come full circle to discipline — to a structured plan. Normally our reason, wills, and emotions should work in that order, but since we so often reverse the order, giving attention to our desires, we must work at directing those desires toward God's will.

When I first began jogging as an exercise, I was unmotivated and therefore inconsistent in doing it. I knew I should jog, that my body needed the physical conditioning, and that I would probably be more healthy as a result. But I was out of condition, it required time I didn't think I had, and above all it was painful. So I started, stopped, started, and stopped, never making consistent progress. Then I read Dr. Kenneth Cooper's book *Aerobics*, which documents the importance of strenuous activities, such as jogging, that exercise the heart. Dr. Cooper explained why jogging was important, gave a few simple guidelines for doing it, and sprinkled his facts and instructions with many illustrations of people whose physical lives were changed dramatically as a result of jogging.

I found myself reading through that book perhaps a half dozen times. I didn't need to be convinced of the importance of jogging; I was already convinced. And I didn't need to reread the few simple rules; they were clear the first time through the book. What I needed was motivation. And those "success" stories — what I call "before and after" stories — motivated me to go out and jog. Reading and rereading them finally succeeded in making me consistent. I influenced my will through my emotions (by motivation) when I could not through my reason (by understanding the importance of jogging).

Now in addition to giving us instructions and guidelines for living, the Bible is filled with "success" stories of real people who trusted God and obeyed Him and whose lives were changed dramatically or who significantly influenced the course of history. The eleventh chapter of Hebrews gives us a brief and partial index of some of these stories. But there are many more not mentioned (as the writer of Hebrews himself acknowledges in Hebrews 11:32). The exploits of men such as Daniel, Nehemiah, and Elijah, as well as Abraham, Noah, and David can motivate us to go and do likewise. So we would do well to constantly include the accounts of some of these men in our Bible reading to motivate us in areas of holiness.

In addition to the Scriptures, we can be alert for the few classic books that really motivate us to a holy and godly life. The number will probably not exceed a half dozen that uniquely meet our needs.[2] These books should be reread frequently just as I reread *Aerobics*. The basic idea is to have a plan — a disciplined approach — that will enable us to stay motivated to holiness.

In the final analysis it is God who works in us to will and to act according to His good purpose. But we are expressly told by Paul to work at this ourselves (Philippians 2:12). Our responsibility regarding our wills is to guard our minds and emotions, being aware of what influences our minds and stimulates our desires. As we do our part, we will see the Spirit of God do His part in making us more holy.

Chapter Fourteen: Habits of Holiness

Just as you used to offer the parts of your body in slavery to impurity and to ever-increasing wickedness, so now offer them in slavery to righteousness leading to holiness.
ROMANS 6:19

The more we sin, the more we are inclined to sin. John Owen expressed it this way, in his quaint seventeenth-century style: "Repeated acts of the consent of the will unto sin may beget a disposition and inclineableness of the will unto a proneness and readiness to consent unto sin upon easy solicitation."[3]

Every sin we commit reinforces the habit of sinning and makes it easier to sin. In the previous chapter we discussed the importance of guarding our minds and emotions, since these faculties are the channels through which the various compelling forces reach our wills. But it is also important that we understand how our habits influence our wills.

Habit is defined as the "prevailing disposition or character of a person's thoughts and feelings."[4] Habits are the thought and emotional patterns engraved on our minds. These internal habit patterns play just as forceful a role as external influences on our actions — in fact, perhaps more so. Owen said, "Every lust is a depraved habit or disposition continually inclining our hearts to do evil."[5]

As unbelievers, we formerly gave ourselves to developing habits of unholiness — what Paul called "ever-increasing wickedness" (Romans 6:19). Every time we sinned — every time we lusted, coveted, hated, cheated, or lied — we were developing habits of ever-increasing wickedness. These repeated acts of

120

unrighteousness became habits that made us, in fact, slaves to sin.

But now, Paul declared, just as we formerly gave ourselves to these wicked habits, so we are to give ourselves to developing habits of holiness (Romans 6:19). We are to put off our old self—our sinful disposition and its habits—and put on the new self—with its character and habits of holiness. To train ourselves in godliness (1 Timothy 4:7) is to discipline and structure our lives so that we develop godly habits. Putting off these sinful habits is what Paul calls mortifying or putting to death the deeds of the body (Romans 8:13).

Though we are to deal with these habits of unholiness, we must not try to do it in our own strength. Breaking sinful habits must be done in cooperation with the Holy Spirit and in dependence upon Him. The determination that "I'll not do that anymore," based upon sheer human resolve, has never once broken the shackles of sin. But there are practical principles which we can follow to train ourselves in godliness.

The first principle is that habits are developed and reinforced by *frequent repetition*. Another definition of habit is "a behavior pattern acquired by frequent repetition."[6] This is the principle underlying the fact that the more we sin the more we are inclined to sin. But the converse is also true. The more we say no to sin, the more we are inclined to say no.

Therefore, in dependence on the Holy Spirit, we must systematically work at acquiring the habit of saying no to the sins that so easily entangle us. We all know what these sins are—the sins to which we are particularly vulnerable. We begin by concentrating on saying no to these. Then God will lead us on to work on other sins which we may not even be aware of at this time. The more we succeed in saying no to our sinful desires, the easier it becomes to say no.

In the same manner we can develop positive habits of holiness. We can develop the habit of thinking thoughts that are pure, true, and good. We can develop the habits of prayer and meditating on the Scriptures. But these habits will only be developed through frequent repetition.

The second principle in breaking sinful habits and acquiring new ones is to *never let an exception occur.* When we allow exceptions we are reinforcing old habits or else failing to reinforce the new one. At this point we must watch the "just this once" type of thinking, which is a subtle, dangerous trap. Because we are unwilling to pay the price of saying no to our desires, we tell ourselves we will indulge only once more and tomorrow will be different. Deep inside we know that tomorrow it will be even more difficult to say no, but we don't dwell on this fact.

The third principle is that *diligence in all areas is required to ensure success in one area.* Owen said, "Without a sincere and diligent effort in every area of obedience, there will be no successful mortification of any one besetting sin."[7] We may feel that a particular habit "isn't too bad," but continually giving in to that habit weakens our wills against the onslaughts of temptation from other directions. This is the reason, for example, that it is so important for us to develop habits of self-control over our physical appetites. We may think indulging these appetites isn't so bad, but such indulgences weaken our wills in every other respect of our lives.

Last, *don't be discouraged by failure.* There is a vast difference between failing and becoming a failure. We become a failure when we give up — when we stop trying. But as long as we are working on those sinful habits, regardless of how often we fail, we have not become a failure, and we can expect to see progress.

It is vain to guard our minds and emotions against that which comes from without if we do not at the same time deal with habits of sin which are within. The battle for holiness must be fought on two fronts — without and within. Only then will we see progress toward holiness.

Holiness and Our Wills

(Chapters 13 and 14)

STUDY QUESTIONS

1. How do the following verses describe our responsibility concerning our reason, emotions, and will?

    *   Romans 6:19

    *   Romans 12:2

    *   Colossians 3:1-2

    *   James 4:7-8

2. Carefully read Proverbs 2:1-12. If we desire to guard our minds from evil, what must we do?

3. List at least two "success" stories from the Bible (see page 119) that especially appeal to you and which you can continually refer to for motivation to holiness.

4. *(For additional study)* Examine how each of these verses relates to holiness and our wills, emotions, or reason. Write down those which are the most meaningful to you, and explain why they are.

   • Genesis 3:1-6; Psalm 1:1-2; John 5:39-40; Ephesians 4:17-19; Philippians 2:12-13; 2 Timothy 2:22

5. Explain in your own words how the reason, emotions, and will are related, and how they work together.

6. Review the four principles for acquiring or breaking a habit listed in chapter 14. Select a habit you want to acquire or break, and write how each of the four principles can help you.

7. What other application of the truths of this session do you want to make in your life?

Holiness and Faith

Read the following portion of *The Pursuit of Holiness*. In the margins, record observations, illustrations, or questions that come to mind as you read. Then answer the study questions that follow the reading.

Chapter Fifteen: Holiness and Faith

By faith Abraham, when called to go to a place he would later receive as his inheritance, obeyed and went, even though he did not know where he was going.
HEBREWS 11:8

Notes and Observations

In the pursuit of holiness Christians are often called on to perform duties that appear unreasonable and even absurd to an unbelieving world. A Christian farmer in Kansas is a case in point. When wheat is exactly ready to be harvested, it is important that the work be completed quickly lest bad weather arise and damage the crop or reduce its quality. Because of this, harvesting is often done on a seven-day-a-week schedule. But this particular farmer, believing Sunday should be observed as the Lord's Day, would never work his harvest crew on Sunday, even when an impending storm threatened. To his neighboring farmers this action appeared strange and unreasonable. Interestingly enough, however, over the years this Christian farmer was the most prosperous in his area. Like Abraham, he obeyed by faith what he believed to be the will of God, even though such obedience must undoubtedly have been difficult at times.[1]

Though we often think of holiness in a more narrow sense of separation from impurity and moral evil, in its broader sense holiness is obedience to the will of God in whatever God directs. It is saying with Jesus, "Here I am . . . I have come to do

127

your will, O God" (Hebrews 10:7). No one can pursue holiness who is not prepared to obey God in every area of his life. The holiness described in the Bible calls us to do more than separate ourselves from the moral pollution of the world around us. It calls us to obey God even when that obedience is costly, when it requires deliberate sacrifice and even exposure to danger.

During my service in the Navy, I was once in charge of an operation where a mishap occurred in which a valuable boat was lost and a dozen or more lives were endangered. It was a situation that could have seriously jeopardized my future naval service. Though the cause of the mishap was mechanical failure, it was also true that we were not conducting the operation exactly according to the rules. During the ensuing investigation, the temptation to protect myself by covering up this fact was extremely strong, but I knew I had to be completely truthful and trust God for the consequences. God blessed that obedience — the investigation focused totally on the mechanical failure, and my career was not harmed.

Obedience to the revealed will of God is often just as much a step of faith as claiming a promise from God. In fact, one of the more intriguing thoughts from the book of Hebrews is the way the writer appears to use obedience and faith interchangeably. For example, he speaks of the Old Testament Hebrews who would never enter God's rest because they *disobeyed* (3:18). Yet they were not able to enter because of their *unbelief* (3:19). This interchange of unbelief and disobedience also occurs later in the book (4:2,6).

These heroes of faith were said to be "still living by faith when they died" (Hebrews 11:13). But we will see that the element of obedience — responding to the will of God — was just as prominent in their lives as was claiming the promises of God. The important point, however, is that they obeyed *by faith*. And since obedience is the pathway to holiness — a holy life being essentially an obedient life — we may say that no one will become holy apart from a life of faith.

Faith is not only necessary to salvation, it is also necessary to live a life pleasing to God. Faith enables us to claim the
promises of God — but it also enables us to obey the commands
of God. Faith enables us to obey when obedience is costly or
seems unreasonable to the natural mind.

Several illustrations from Hebrews 11, the great "faith" chapter, bring out this truth. For example, by faith Abel offered to
God a better sacrifice than Cain did, and through this received
God's approval (verse 4). We can assume that God had revealed
to Cain and Abel the duty of offering sacrifices and the acceptable way of performing that duty. It is apparent from the rest
of Scripture that God's acceptable way was through the sacrifice of a lamb — through the shedding of blood. Now *by faith* Abel
believed what God said. He took Him at His word and obeyed,
even though it is likely he did not understand why the sacrifice
of the lamb was the only acceptable sacrifice. Cain, on the other
hand, did not believe God's revelation regarding an acceptable sacrifice — perhaps because it did not appear reasonable to
him — so he did not obey and thus failed to obtain God's blessing.

The world's values surround us on every hand. Fame,
fortune, and present happiness are held as the most desirable goals in life. But the Bible flatly contradicts the value of
these goals: "Whoever wants to be great among you must be
your servant, and whoever wants to be first must be your slave"
(Matthew 20:26-27). The rich should not "put their hope in
wealth, which is so uncertain," but are told to hope in God,
"to be rich in good deeds and to be generous and willing to
share" (1 Timothy 6:17-18). It takes faith to pursue such biblical values when the society around us is pursuing goals that
are totally opposite. This faith focuses on believing that God
ultimately upholds and blesses those who obey Him, and who
trust Him for the consequences of obedience.

Noah's life is an example of this kind of faith: "By faith
Noah, when warned about things not yet seen, in holy fear
built an ark to save his family. By his faith he condemned the

129

world and became heir of the righteousness that comes by faith" (Hebrews 11:7). God's revelation to Noah concerning the forthcoming judgment on the world was first of all a warning. By faith Noah believed that warning. He had conviction about things not yet seen based solely upon the revealed Word of God. Noah also had confidence that the way of salvation from the impending judgment was through God's appointed means — the ark. He responded to that promise, and so saved both himself and his family.

Noah's building of the ark may well be considered one of the greatest examples the world has ever witnessed of perseverance in a difficult duty of obedience. For 140 years he labored because he both heeded the warning of God and believed the promise of God.

Abraham's life also illustrates the obedience element of faith. The call of Abraham consisted of two parts — a command and a promise. The command was to leave his father's house and go to a land God would show him. The promise was that God would make of him a great nation and through him bless all the families of the earth. Abraham believed that both the command and the promise came from God, so he obeyed the command and expected fulfillment of the promise. It is recorded of him, "By faith Abraham . . . obeyed" (Hebrews 11:8).

The Bible records the story of Abraham's faith and obedience in such a matter-of-fact way that we can easily overlook the difficulty of his obedience and the faith it required. John Brown likens the case of Abraham to "a person, previous to the discovery of America, leaving the shores of Europe, and committing himself and his family to the mercy of the waves, in consequence of a command of God and a promise that they should be conducted to a country where he should become the founder of a great nation, and the source of blessing to many nations."[2]

The path of obedience in the pursuit of holiness is often contrary to human reason. If we do not have *conviction* in the necessity of obeying the revealed will of God as well as *confi-*

130

dence in the promises of God, we will never persevere in this difficult pursuit. We must have conviction that it is God's will that we seek holiness — regardless of how arduous and painful the seeking may be. And we must be confident that the pursuit of holiness results in God's approval and blessing, even when circumstances make it appear otherwise.

Often in our lives a specific act of obedience will require both conviction and confidence. God's commandments to Israel to keep the sabbatical year was one such instance. He commanded that every seventh year the land should have a sabbath rest to the Lord, during which no sowing or pruning was to be done (Leviticus 25:3-4). Along with this command God promised that He would bless their crops in the sixth year so that they would have enough to eat till crops in the eighth year were harvested (Leviticus 25:20-22). Only as the Israelites had confidence in the promise of God would they dare to obey the command of God. Sadly, the Old Testament record seems to indicate they had neither the confidence in God's promise nor the conviction that His revealed will on this matter was important to their national and spiritual prosperity.

A New Testament application of this spiritual principle is found in the words of Jesus, "But seek first his kingdom and his righteousness, and all these things will be given to you as well" (Matthew 6:33). The command is to seek God's kingdom first. The promise is that as we do, God will provide for our temporal needs. Because we are often fainthearted regarding the promise of God, we find it difficult to obey His command. Consequently we often give the affairs of this life top priority in the basic decisions of our lives.

Jeroboam, the first king of the Northern Kingdom of Israel, also illustrates how lack of faith leads to disobedience. God promised: "If you do whatever I command you and walk in my ways and do what is right in my eyes by keeping my statutes and commands as David my servant did, I will be with you. I will build you a dynasty as enduring as the one I built for David and will give Israel to you" (1 Kings 11:38).

Did Jeroboam believe God and obey Him? We read that he did not:

> Jeroboam thought to himself, "The kingdom will now likely revert to the house of David. If these people go up to offer sacrifices at the temple of the Lord in Jerusalem, they will again give their allegiance to their lord, Rehoboam king of Judah. They will kill me and return to King Rehoboam." After seeking advice, the king made two golden calves. He said to the people, "It is too much for you to go up to Jerusalem. Here are your gods, O Israel, who brought you up out of Egypt." (1 Kings 12:26-28)

We could well think that Jeroboam had not even heard God's command and promise, so flagrantly did he disregard them. He certainly heard, but the message he heard was of no value to him because it was not combined with faith (Hebrews 4:2). But before we condemn Jeroboam, let us consider our own lives. How often do we fail to obey God's clearly revealed will because we do not exercise faith?

Because we do not believe that humility is the path to God's exaltation (1 Peter 5:6), we jockey for a place of position and power in our relations with others. Because we do not believe that God takes note of and will in His time avenge all wrongs done to us (Romans 12:19), we study in our own minds how we can "get back" at someone we feel has wronged us. Because we are not convinced of the deceitfulness of sin (Hebrews 3:13), we play with it, thinking we will thereby find satisfaction. And because we do not have a firm conviction that "without holiness no one will see the Lord" (Hebrews 12:14), we do not seriously pursue holiness as a priority in our lives.

Faith and holiness are inextricably linked. Obeying the commands of God usually involves believing the promises of

God. One definition of faith might be "Obeying the revealed will of God and trusting Him for the results."

"Without faith it is impossible to please God" (Hebrews 11:6). If we would pursue holiness we must have faith to obey the will of God revealed in the Scripture and faith to believe that the promises of God will then be ours.

Holiness and Faith

(Chapter 15)

STUDY QUESTIONS

1. Explain the relationship you see between faith and obedience in Hebrews 3:17-19 and 4:2,6.

2. Read through Hebrews 11, noting the instances of obedience by faith. List five things which some of the persons mentioned in this chapter believed. Which is the most meaningful for you, and why?

3. List five ways in which the persons mentioned in Hebrews 11 obeyed God. Which is the most challenging example for you, and why?

4. *(For additional study)* Review the principles given in the following verses. Explain how faith is required to follow each one, and under what circumstances the principle would be the most difficult for you to believe.

    *   Matthew 20:26-27; Luke 6:30-31; Romans 12:19; 1 Timothy 6:17-18; Hebrews 3:13

5. We have seen holiness defined as the state of being "morally blameless" (page 13), "conformity to the moral precepts of the Bible" (page 13), "conformity to the character of God" (page 17), and "obedience to the will of God in whatever God directs" (page 127). From what you have learned in this and the previous sessions,

write a summary definition of holiness which is meaningful to you, then compare it with the definition you wrote in session 1, question 5.

6. What application of the truths of this session do you want to make in your life?

Holiness in an Unholy World

Read the following portion of *The Pursuit of Holiness*. In the margins, record observations, illustrations, or questions that come to mind as you read. Then answer the study questions that follow the reading.

Chapter Sixteen: Holiness in an Unholy World

My prayer is not that you take them out of the world but that you protect them from the evil one.
JOHN 17:15

Notes and Observations

All believers must live their Christian lives in the context of an unholy world. Some face extraordinary temptation as they live in the midst of a flagrantly sinful atmosphere. The student in the university dormitory or the man or woman on a military base or aboard ship must often live in an environment polluted with sensuality, wantonness, and lust. The businessman or woman is often under tremendous pressure to compromise ethical and legal standards to satisfy the greed and dishonesty of associates. Unless the Christian is prepared for such evil assaults on his mind and heart, he will have great difficulty maintaining personal holiness.

James said that part of true religion consists in keeping ourselves "from being polluted by the world" (James 1:27), and Paul urged us to "come out from them and be separate" (2 Corinthians 6:17). How should the believer respond when he finds himself surrounded on every hand by the unrelenting pressures of a sinful world?

It is clear from our Lord's prayer that He does not intend for us to withdraw from contact with the world of non-Christians (John 17:15). Instead, He said we are to be "the salt of the earth" and "the light of the world" (Matthew 5:13-14). The writers of the New Testament take it for granted that Christians will live in the midst of an unholy world. (See such passages as 1 Corinthians 5:9-10; Philippians 2:14-15; 1 Peter 2:12, and 3:15-16.) And we are never told that it will be easy to live in a godless environment. Instead, we are warned to expect ridicule and abuse (John 15:19; 2 Timothy 3:12; 1 Peter 4:3-4).

Instead of withdrawing from contact with the world, we must strive to resist its influence. To do this we must first of all resolve to live by the convictions God has given us from His Word. We cannot be like Mr. Talkative in *Pilgrim's Progress* who prided himself on being adaptable to any kind of company and any kind of talk. He was like a chameleon who changes his color every time he changes his environment. Some of us have known people who had two vocabularies — one among Christians and another among their associates of the world.

The convictions we develop about God's will for a holy life must be rock-ribbed enough to withstand the ridicule of the ungodly and the pressures they put on us to conform to their unholy ways. I still remember the taunts of my fellow officers aboard ship who teased me unmercifully about a large obscene picture they had prominently displayed in the officers' dining room.

One helpful reinforcement to living according to our convictions is to identify ourselves with Christ openly, wherever we find ourselves in the world. This must be done in a gracious yet clear-cut manner. Going aboard a new ship, I sought to identify myself as a Christian by the simple, wordless act of carrying my Bible openly when going ashore on "liberty." A student in a university dormitory can do the same thing by leaving his Bible out to be seen by all who come into his room. This open identification with Christ helps to spare us from the temptation of adapting to our sinful environment as Mr. Talkative did.

But even though we resolve to live in the world by the convictions God has given us from His Word, and we openly identify ourselves with Christ, we still are often subjected to the pollution of unholy surroundings. The lewd pictures everywhere, the obscene jokes told in our presence, and the endless recounting and boasting of immoral activities by those who do them, all serve to drag our minds down into the filth of this world. To this list we could add the dishonest shortcuts taken by business associates, the constant gossiping of our neighbors and coworkers, and the lies and half-truths we hear all around us.

The Bible is our best defense against this pollution. David said, "How can a young man keep his way pure? By living according to your word" (Psalm 119:9). The Bible will cleanse our minds of the defilement of the world if we meditate on its teachings. It will also serve as a continual warning to us not to succumb to frequent temptations to indulge our eyes and thoughts in the immorality around us. I know a man who attended a godless, humanistic university. To guard his mind from the corrupting influences of that environment, he determined to spend as much time in the Word of God as he did in his studies. Today that man is a missionary leader who has had a profound impact on hundreds of lives.

Such passages of Scripture as "Hell and destruction are never full; so the eyes of man are never satisfied" (Proverbs 27:20, KJV), and "Nor should there be obscenity, foolish talk, or coarse joking, which are out of place, but rather thanksgiving" (Ephesians 5:4) are verses we can memorize and meditate on as we find ourselves in corrupt surroundings.

Our reaction to the sinful world around us, however, must be more than just defensive. We must be concerned not only for our own purity of mind and heart, but also for the eternal destiny of those who would pollute us. God has left us in the world to be both salt and light (Matthew 5:13-14). The use of salt as a metaphor to describe our relationship to the world teaches us that Christians are to be a preserving power, an antiseptic, an agent to prevent and retard decay. Dr. William Hendriksen says, "Salt combats deterioration. Similarly Christians, by showing themselves to be Christians indeed, are constantly combatting moral and spiritual decay. . . . To be sure, the world is wicked. Yet God alone knows how *far more* corrupt it would be without the restraining example, life, and prayers of the saints."[1]

As the "light of the world" we are the bearers of the good news of salvation. Jesus Himself is the true light and, just as it was said of John the Baptist, we are to be "a witness to testify concerning that light" (John 1:7-9). A Christian who witnesses in a spirit of genuine concern for another person is not likely to be corrupted by that person's immorality. And through gracious, loving concern, he may perhaps win that person to the Savior.

We do not act as the salt of the earth or shine as the light of the world by necessarily denouncing the sins of our worldly associates. Our own holy life will serve as a sufficient rebuke, and our interest in others at this point is not their conduct but their need of Jesus Christ as their Savior. Henry Clay Trumbull was, among other things, a great personal evangelist. One day he found himself seated on a train next to a young man who was drinking quite heavily. Each time the young man opened his bottle, he offered a drink to Mr. Trumbull, who declined with thanks. Finally the young man said to Mr. Trumbull, "You must think I'm a pretty rough fellow." Mr. Trumbull's gracious reply, "I think you're a very generous-hearted fellow," opened the way for an earnest conversation with the young man about his need to commit himself to Christ.[2]

After Jesus called Matthew the tax collector to Himself and was eating in Matthew's house with a number of his friends, the Pharisees complained, "Why do you eat and drink with tax collectors and sinners?" Jesus answered them, "It is not the healthy who need a doctor, but the sick. I have not come to call the righteous, but sinners to repentance" (Luke 5:30-32). Surely this is what God would have us do as we shine as lights in the world.

Finally, despite all the suggestions in this session, there may be a time when the corrupt environment becomes intolerable; where we, like Lot, become tormented by the lawless deeds we see and hear (2 Peter 2:7-8; Genesis 19). Such a situation may occur, for example, in a coed dormitory where unmarried couples are living in open immorality, or in a business situation where there is unceasing pressure to break the law or compromise Christian principles. In these circumstances, we should prayerfully consider the need to leave that ungodly situation. (I realize this may not be humanly possible in a military situation, but we can resort to prayer, since with God all things are possible.)

Maintaining personal holiness in an unholy world is admittedly difficult. The foregoing suggestions are not intended to make the problem seem easy, but to offer some practical help for a tough problem. Above all, we must look to Jesus who, though He ate with tax collectors and sinners, was Himself "holy, blameless, pure, set apart from sinners, exalted above the heavens" (Hebrews 7:26). And we must claim His promise that "No temptation has seized you except what is common to man. And God is faithful; he will not let you be tempted beyond what you can bear. But when you are tempted, he will also provide a way out so that you can stand up under it" (1 Corinthians 10:13).

Notes and Observations

Chapter Seventeen: The Joy of Holiness
For the kingdom of God is not a matter of eating and drinking, but of righteousness, peace and joy in the Holy Spirit.
ROMANS 14:17

God intends the Christian life to be a life of joy — not drudgery. The idea that holiness is associated with a dour disposition is a caricature of the worst sort. In fact, just the opposite is true. Only those who walk in holiness experience true joy.

Jesus said, "If you obey my commands, you will remain in my love, just as I have obeyed my Father's commands and remain in his love. I have told you this so that my joy may be in

Notes and Observations

you and that your joy may be complete" (John 15:10-11). In this statement Jesus links obedience and joy in a cause and effect manner; that is, joy results from obedience. Only those who are obedient — who are pursuing holiness as a way of life — will know the joy that comes from God.

In what way does holiness produce joy? For one thing, there is the joy of *fellowship with God*. David said, "You will fill me with joy in your presence, with eternal pleasures at your right hand" (Psalm 16:11). True joy comes only from God, and He shares this joy with those who walk in fellowship with Him. When David committed the awful sins of adultery and murder, he lost his sense of God's joy because he lost fellowship with God. After this, in his penitential prayer he asked God to "restore to me the joy of your salvation" (Psalm 51:12). A life of disobedience cannot be a life of joy.

The daily experience of Christ's love is linked to our obedience to Him. It is not that His love is *conditioned* on our obedience. That would be legalism. But our *experience* of His love is dependent upon our obedience.

Dr. William Hendriksen observes that God's love both precedes and follows our obedience. God's love, he says, "by *preceding* our love . . . creates in us the eager desire to keep Christ's precepts; then, by *following* our love, it rewards us for keeping them."[3]

Another cause of joy is knowing that I am obeying God — that I am no longer resisting Him in some particular area of my life. This joy is especially apparent when, after a long struggle between the Spirit and our sinful natures, we have by His grace finally and radically dealt with some besetting sin that had previously mastered us. We might call this the joy of victory; I prefer to call it the joy of obedience.

In addition to the joy of fellowship with the Holy God, a holy life also produces the joy of *anticipated reward*. The writer of Hebrews said, "Let us throw off everything that hinders and the sin that so easily entangles, and let us run with perseverance the race marked out for us. Let us fix our eyes on

Jesus, the Author and Perfecter of our faith, who *for the joy set before him* endured the cross, scorning its shame, and sat down at the right hand of the throne of God" (Hebrews 12:1-2, emphasis added). Jesus was motivated to endure by anticipating the joy of His reward. No amount of hardship and struggle could deprive Him of that anticipation.

In the parable of the talents, the Lord said to the two servants who used their talents, "Well done, thou good and faithful servant. . . . Enter thou into the joy of thy Lord" (Matthew 25:21,23, KJV). One of the "talents" God has given to every Christian is the possibility of walking in holiness, being free from the dominion of sin. We, too, can look forward to entering into the joy of the Lord as we walk in holiness to the end of our days.

Joy not only *results* from a holy life, but there is also a sense in which joy helps *produce* a holy life. Nehemiah said to the dispirited exiles who returned to Jerusalem, "The joy of the Lord is your strength" (Nehemiah 8:10). The Christian living in disobedience also lives devoid of joy and hope. But when he begins to understand that Christ has delivered him from the reign of sin, when he begins to see that he is united to Him who has all power and authority, and that it is possible to walk in obedience, he begins to have hope. And as he hopes in Christ, he begins to have joy. In the strength of this joy he begins to overcome the sins that so easily entangle him. He then finds that the joy of a holy walk is infinitely more satisfying than the fleeting pleasures of sin.

But to experience this joy, we must make some choices. We must choose to forsake sin, not only because it is defeating to us, but because it grieves the heart of God. We must choose to count on the fact that we are dead to sin, freed from its reign and dominion, and we can now actually say no to sin. We must choose to accept our responsibility to discipline our lives for obedience.

God has provided all we need for our pursuit of holiness. He has delivered us from the reign of sin and given us His indwelling Holy Spirit. He has revealed His will for holy living in His Word, and He works in us to will and to act according to His good purpose. He has sent pastors and teachers to exhort and encourage us in the path of holiness; and He answers our prayers when we cry to Him for strength against temptation.

Truly the choice is ours. What will we choose? Will we accept our responsibility and discipline ourselves to live in habitual obedience to the will of God? Will we persevere in the face of frequent failure, resolving never to give up? Will we decide that personal holiness is worth the price of saying no to our body's demands to indulge its appetites?

In the Preface we considered the farmer who, in dependence on God, fulfills his responsibility to produce a harvest. He does not sit back and wait for God to act; rather he acts himself, trusting God to do His part. If we are to attain any measure of holiness we must have a similar attitude. God has clearly said, "Be holy, because I am holy."

Surely He has not commanded us to be holy without providing the means to be holy. The privilege of being holy is yours, and the decision and responsibility to be holy is yours. If you make that decision, you will experience the fullness of joy which Christ has promised to those who walk in obedience to Him.

Holiness in an Unholy World

(Chapters 16 and 17)

STUDY QUESTIONS

1. After studying the following verses, summarize what they teach about the Christian's relationship to an unholy world.

    • Matthew 5:13-14; John 17:14-16; 1 Peter 3:15-16

2. From the following verses, explain what the Christian's response should be when he is ridiculed or abused for his holy life.

    • Matthew 5:11-12; John 15:19; 2 Timothy 3:12; 1 Peter 2:12; 4:12-13

3. How can we follow the example of Jesus in associating with unholy people (read Luke 5:29-32) and at the same time keep ourselves holy as He did (Hebrews 7:26)? List some actual situations you might face in which this would be difficult.

4. Read 1 Corinthians 10:13. How can this promise help you in some unholy environment you may be in?

5. *(For additional study)* Examine how each of the following verses relates to holiness in an unholy world, or to the joy of holiness. Write down those which are the most helpful to you, and explain why they are.

    • Psalm 51:10-12; 1 Corinthians 5:9-10; Ephesians 5:5-12; Philippians 2:14-15; Hebrews 12:1-2; 1 Peter 4:3-4; 2 Peter 2:7-9

6. What does each of the following verses teach about the joy of a holy life?

    •   Nehemiah 8:9-10

    •   Psalm 16:11

    •   John 15:10-11

    •   Romans 14:17

7.   What application of the truths of this session do you want to make in your life?

A Further Word

In Ephesians 4:20-24, Paul urges us to put off our old self and to put on the new self. To put off the old self is to deal with sin patterns in our lives. To put on the new self is to develop Christlike character traits such as love, compassion, generosity, and forgiveness.

The Pursuit of Holiness deals largely with putting off the old self—dealing with sin in our lives. A sequel to this book is available that focuses on putting on the new self—the development of Christian character. It is just as important that we put on the new self as it is that we put off the old. Therefore, I encourage you to consider the sequel book, *The Practice of Godliness*. It is available by contacting NavPress at P. O. Box 35002, Colorado Springs, Colorado 80935, www.navpress.com.

Help for Group Leaders

The following pages are designed to help a discussion leader guide a group through this book. You can appoint one person to lead each session, or you can rotate leadership.

GETTING STARTED

Choose a time and place to meet that is consistent, comfortable, and relatively free from distractions. If you meet in a home, make plans to deal with pets, ringing telephones, and other distractions.

SET YOUR SESSION FORMAT.

Decide how long your sessions will be, and map out a general plan for each gathering. Following is a sample format for a sixty-minute session.

- *Ten minutes* for settling in, opening prayer, and warm-up conversation. Refreshments can help people mingle, but don't let them consume too much of your time.
- *Forty minutes* for discussion of the study questions. Open your discussion by inviting group members to share their responses to the chapter(s) they read during the week. Then move into discussing the questions that followed the session's reading.
- *Ten minutes* for closing comments and prayer time. Before you end, call attention to the next session's readings and encourage group members to complete the study questions on their own.

CUSTOMIZE THE MATERIAL FOR YOUR GROUP.

In this study guide, you'll find the following elements.

- *Text.* Each session opens with the chapters in *The Pursuit of Holiness* to be read before gathering. You'll want to call attention to the next session's assigned readings at the close of each meeting.
- *Study questions.* Participants are encouraged to work through the corresponding study questions prior to each group session.
- *For Additional Study question(s).* These extra questions are for additional study and discussion if time allows. You can draw from these questions if more material is needed, or encourage group members to study them on their own as a follow-up after the session.
- *Application question.* The final question in each session invites group members to consider how they would apply the truths of this study to their lives. Encourage participants to talk with God about the application and plan their applications in connection with Him. Taking the time to respond prayerfully will enhance their personal understanding and life transformation.

Leaders should decide which questions to cover during group time. You probably will not have time to discuss all questions in depth; focus on the ones that are most important for your group. When a question is about a Scripture passage, it will be helpful to read the passage together. When there are a number of passages, decide which ones to discuss during group time.

Please note that the number of sessions in the study guide doesn't correlate directly with the number of chapters in the book, and that the study guide sometimes combines two book chapters into a session. We created the study this way to compress the sessions into a shorter amount of time (twelve weeks, if you do one session per week) than the book would allow (seventeen chapters). If you want to create a longer study, you might cover some sessions in two weeks instead of one.

PLAN YOUR FIRST SESSION.

You may want to plan a potluck for your first meeting together. In this way, group members can get to know one another in the context of a meal, which is a good way to break down barriers. Then after dinner you can have your first session.

The content you cover in this session depends on which of the following options you choose.

Option one: A twelve-week study. This is how we've set up the study. In this format, make sure each participant has a copy of this book before session 1. Encourage everyone to read the chapters and respond to the study questions for session 1 prior to your first meeting.

Option two: A thirteen-week study. In this option, you add an additional "opening week" to use for distributing the books and getting acquainted with group members. In this session, have someone read aloud the first two and a half pages of the preface as the group follows along. (You can stop your reading with the paragraph that ends, "That is why we will always be pursuing—as opposed to attaining—holiness in this life.") Encourage participants to talk about their responses to what Jerry Bridges is saying. Talk together about group members' expectations for the study. Are they anticipating the topic or are they intimidated by talking about holiness? What connotations come to mind when they think of holiness? Pray together for open hearts and minds; for an awareness that God is present, engaged, and interested in your discussions; and for a spirit of mutual encouragement as you study and discuss the book during the coming weeks. Then assign the preparation under option one above for your next meeting—the real "session 1" of this study.

Whichever option you choose, be sure to set aside adequate time in the first meeting for people to share who they are. It is amazing how much more productive and honest a Bible discussion is when the participants know each other.

At some point in the evening (probably toward the end), go over the following guidelines. They help make a discussion more fruitful, especially when you are dealing with issues that truly matter to people.

- *Trustworthiness and respect.* No one should repeat what someone shares in the group unless that person gives express permission. Even then, discretion is imperative. Be trustworthy. Participants should talk about their own feelings and experiences, not those of others.
- *Attendance.* Each session builds on the previous ones, and you need each other. So, ask group members to commit to attending all sessions, unless an emergency arises.
- *Participation.* This is a *group* discussion, not a lecture. It is important that each person participate in some way.
- *Preparation.* Encourage everyone to read the material and answer the questions

before the group meets. Your discussions will be more interesting if group members have prepared in advance. In addition, group members will get far more out of the study if they have spent time thinking about the questions and meditating on the Scriptures before meeting.

- *Honesty.* Appropriate openness is a key to a good group. Be who you really are, not who you think you ought to be.
- *Transformation.* The goal of this study is to come to know God's heart and character in a way that leads to transformation from the inside out. As you read and study, please allow God to take you past simply gaining knowledge to encountering Him in fresh ways.

GENERAL HELPS

Below, we have provided general helps for leading your group, but we can't cover every situation you will encounter—such as a group that talks too much or a group that won't discuss at all. Talk with veteran leaders in your church when you need input and ideas. And remember: Your greatest help is always God's Holy Spirit, who has committed to living with you and doing life with you. He's an extraordinary teacher, and you can rely on His strength, wisdom, and problem-solving skills for your group.

PREPARING FOR A SESSION

Your aim as a leader is to prepare an environment that is conducive to growth. You want group members to feel comfortable with one another so they freely engage with the material and discussion.

Pray for the group. As the group leader, your most important preparation for each session is prayer. You will want to make your prayers personal, of course, but here are some suggestions for how to pray:

- Let God be the leader of the group. Ask Him to show you what portions and questions to emphasize and how to format the discussion. Invite God to give you input on your group's unique needs each week.
- Ask the Holy Spirit to bring to life the truths you are studying, personalizing them for each group member.
- Pray that nothing will keep the group members from attending. Ask God to

enable them to feel free to share their thoughts and feelings honestly and to contribute their unique gifts and insights.

- Pray for group members' private times with God this week. Ask God to be active in nurturing them.
- Ask for the Holy Spirit's guidance in exercising patience, acceptance, sensitivity, and wisdom as you talk with each other. Pray for an atmosphere of genuine love in the group, with each member being open to learning and change.
- Pray that your discussion will lead each of you to love the Lord more deeply, obey Him more closely, and demonstrate His presence more tangibly.
- Pray for insight as you go over the study materials and for wisdom as you lead the group so that you tap into God's desires for your time together.

Study and customize the material. After prayer, your most important preparation is to be thoroughly familiar with the material you will discuss. You will find it important to read the chapter(s) that is covered by each session and to make sure you have answered all of the questions.

Decide which questions you want to discuss as a group. You may not have time to cover all the questions. Consider and ask God about which questions are most important for your particular group.

LEADING A SESSION

Following are general guidelines for leading a group discussion. If you are a new leader, you can also ask an experienced group leader to mentor you.

Invite God to be the leader. Open each session with prayer, acknowledging that God is present with the group and that He has an "agenda" for the session. Surrender your plan for the time to Him and invite Him to work in and speak to group members.

Work toward a relaxed and open atmosphere. This may not come quickly, so be a model for the others of acceptance, openness to truth and change, and love. Develop a genuine interest in each person's remarks and expect to learn from them. Show that you care by listening carefully. Be affirming.

Invite opening comments. Open your discussion by inviting group members to share any responses, observations, or questions about the chapter(s) they read. If a group member brings up a point that will be discussed later in the session, affirm what a good point it is and mention that you'll be talking more about this later. This will help keep your discussion from getting sidetracked at the beginning.

Pay attention to how you ask the questions. Don't ask flatly, "What did you get for number 1?" Instead, by your tone of voice, convey your interest and enthusiasm for the question and your warmth toward the group. The group will adopt your attitude. Read the questions as though you were asking them of good friends.

Vary your approach as you move through the questions. For some questions, you might pose the issue to no one in particular and wait for responses. For others, you might direct the question to a specific individual, let him or her respond, and then encourage others to respond as well. As much as time permits, encourage unrushed multiple responses. Sometimes you'll discover deeper levels of insight as one participant builds upon the thoughts of another.

Expect variations or pauses in the discussion. Sometimes a group won't respond as quickly as you'd like. If that happens:

- Be comfortable with silence. Let the group wrestle to think of answers. Don't be quick to jump in and rescue the group with your answers.
- Reword a question if the group members have trouble understanding it.
- If a question evokes little response, feel free to leave it and move on.
- Feel free to answer questions yourself occasionally. In particular, you might need to be the first one to answer questions about personal experiences. In this way you will model the depth of openness and thought you hope others will show. You can also model an appropriate length of response. Don't answer every question, but don't be a silent observer.
- If the discussion is winding down on a question, go on to the next one. It's not necessary to push people to see every possible angle.

Ask only one question at a time. Often, participants' responses will suggest a follow-up question to you. Be discerning as to when you are following a fruitful train of thought and when you are going off on a tangent.

Be aware of time. Don't spend so much time discussing that you run out of time for application and prayer. Your goal is not to have something to discuss but to become more like Jesus Christ.

Encourage constructive controversy. The group can learn a lot from struggling with the many sides of an issue. If you aren't threatened when someone disagrees, the whole group will be more open and vulnerable. Intervene, if necessary, to be sure that people are debating ideas and interpretations of Scripture, not attacking each other's feelings and character. If the group gets stuck in an irresolvable argument, say something such as, "We can agree to disagree here," and move on.

Don't be the expert. People will stop talking if they feel you are judging their answers or that you think you know best. Let God's words in the Bible be the expert, the final say. Let people candidly express their feelings and experiences.

Don't do for the group what it can do for itself. With a beginning group, you may have to ask all of the questions, do all of the outside research, plan the applications, etc. But within a few meetings you should start delegating various leadership responsibilities. Let members learn to exercise their gifts. Let them start making decisions and solving problems together. Encourage them to maturity and unity in Christ.

Encourage people to share feelings as well as facts. There are two dimensions of truth: the truth about how people feel, and the truth about who God is. People need to face both their real feelings and the real God.

Summarize the discussion frequently. Help the group see where the discussion is going.

Let the group plan applications. The action responses in this study are suggestions. Your group should adapt them so they are relevant and life-changing for members. If group members aren't committed to an application, they won't do it. Encourage, but don't force.

Allow freedom during your prayer times. To close a meeting, you can have one person pray or open up the time for brief conversational prayers from anyone who wishes to pray aloud. (Tip: No one should ever feel pressured or obligated to pray aloud. It can help everyone relax if you assure them of this ahead of time.) You might use your prayer time to pray for group members' general needs, or suggest that you pray personally for each member regarding the insights and struggles he or she encountered with this session. Feel free to allow silence during prayer so that God has space to respond individually to group members' prayers.

REVIEWING AFTER A SESSION

Use the following questions each week to help you improve your leadership next time:

1. How did you see God at work during your time together?
2. Did you have the right number of questions prepared? Should you add to the next session's questions or plan to cover fewer questions?
3. Did you discuss the major issues? If you missed major points, on your notes

for next week mark the essential questions or points you want to cover and summarize.

4. Did you know your material thoroughly enough to have freedom in leading?

5. Did you keep the discussion from wandering?

6. Did everyone participate? Were people open? Was anyone overtalkative? Disruptive? Think about how you can handle these problems next week if they occur again, or ask another group leader for ideas.

7. Was the discussion practical? Did it lead to new understanding, new hope, repentance, change? If necessary, brainstorm some application questions that can help lead the group in this direction.

8. Did you begin and end on time? If necessary, put a clock or watch in plain sight in your meeting area so you can easily glance at it and keep track of time.

9. Did you give the group the maximum responsibility that it can handle?

10. What does God think of the time together?

11. How would He want to be your coach and mentor as you lead next week? If you're feeling inadequate in some area of leadership, how would He want to be strong for you and provide the power, wisdom, and expertise you need?

12. How does He want to affirm you for your investment in leading this group? Where is He proud of you and pleased with you, as a proud Father might be?

Notes

SESSION ONE: **Holiness Is for You**

1. *Strong's Exhaustive Concordance of the Bible* (New York: Abingdon Press, 1890), p. 7 of the "Greek Dictionary of the New Testament."

2. W. E. Vine, *An Expository Dictionary of New Testament Words* (1940; single volume edition, London: Oliphants, Ltd., 1957), pp. 225-226.

3. William S. Plumer, *Psalms* (1867; reprint edition, Edinburgh: The Banner of Truth Trust, 1975), p. 557.

4. J. C. Ryle, *Holiness* (1952 edition, London: James Clarke & Co.), p. viii.

5. Andrew Bonar, *A Commentary on Leviticus* (1846; reprint edition, Edinburgh: The Banner of Truth Trust, 1972), p. 218.

6. Holiness "is characteristically Godlikeness" (G. B. Stevens, in *Hastings Bible Dictionary*, as quoted by W. E. Vine in *An Expository Dictionary of New Testament Words*, p. 227). Charles Hodge, writing on the phrase in Romans 6:19, *righteousness unto holiness*, said, "The proximate result of obedience to God is inward conformity to the Divine image" (*Commentary on the Epistle to the Romans* [1886; reprint edition, Grand Rapids, Mich.: Wm. B. Eerdmans Publishing Co., 1955], p. 209). A. W. Pink said, "Holiness . . . consists of that internal change or renovation of our souls whereby our minds, affections and wills are brought into harmony with God" (*The Doctrine of Sanctification* [Swengel, Pa.: Bible Truth Depot, 1955], p. 25).

7. Attributes as applied to God refer to His essential qualities and are inferred from Scriptures describing God. His attribute of holiness is taken from such passages as Exodus 15:11; Leviticus 19:2; Psalm 89:35; Isaiah 57:15; and 1 Peter 1:15-16.

8. Stephen Charnock, *The Existence and Attributes of God* (reprint edition, Evansville, Ind.: Sovereign Grace Book Club, 1958), p. 449.

9. For examples see Psalm 89:18; Isaiah 40:25; 43:14; Hosea 11:9; Habakkuk 3:3; Jeremiah 51:5; and Ezekiel 39:7.

10. Charnock, *Existence and Attributes*, p. 448.

SESSION TWO: **Holiness Is Not an Option**

1. J. C. Ryle, *Holiness* (1952 edition, London: James Clarke & Co.), p. xv.
2. Walter Marshall; 1692, quoted in A. W. Pink, *The Doctrine of Sanctification* (Swengel, Pa.: Bible Truth Depot, 1955), p. 29.

SESSION THREE: **The Holiness of Christ**

1. John Brown, *Expository Discourses on 1 Peter* (1848; reprint edition, Edinburgh: The Banner of Truth Trust, Volume 1), p. 106.

SESSION FOUR: **The Battle for Holiness**

1. I am indebted to Dr. D. Martyn Lloyd Jones for his helpful exposition of the term "died to sin" in chapter 2 of his book *Romans: An Exposition of Chapter 6 — The New Man* (Edinburgh: The Banner of Truth Trust, 1972).
2. John Murray, *The Epistle to the Romans, The New International Commentary on the New Testament* (Grand Rapids, Mich.: Wm. B. Eerdmans Publishing Co., 1968), p. 213. Used by permission.
3. From *Godliness Through Discipline* by Jay E. Adams, p. 6. Reprinted 1973 by Baker Book House and used by permission.
4. Lloyd-Jones, *Romans: An Exposition of Chapter 6*, pp. 152-153.
5. Adapted from the definition of the heart by the Puritan John Owen in his treatise *Indwelling Sin* (1656) as it appears in *Temptation and Sin* (reprint edition, Evansville, Ind.: Sovereign Grace Book Club, 1958), p. 170.
6. This idea is taken from comments on James 1:14 by the Puritan James Manton in *An Exposition on the Epistle of James* (1693; reprint edition, Sovereign Grace Publishers, 1962), p. 93.
7. Owen, *Temptation and Sin*, p. 199.

SESSION FIVE: **God's Provision and Our Responsibility**

1. I am indebted to Dr. D. Martyn Lloyd Jones for his helpful exposition of the term "died to sin" in chapter 2 of his book *Romans: An Exposition of Chapter 6 — The New Man* (Edinburgh: The Banner of Truth Trust, 1972), p. 144.
2. It is also true that the Holy Spirit is the divine Agent who has made us alive to God (John 6:63). But we are here considering the results of being delivered from the realm of sin into the realm of God, and the indwelling of the Holy Spirit is one of the results.

3. D. Martyn Lloyd-Jones, *The Sons of God — Exposition of Romans 8:5-17* (Edinburgh: The Banner of Truth Trust, 1974), p. 124.

4. Lloyd-Jones, p. 136.

Session Six: **Putting Sin to Death**

1. By permission. From *Webster's New Collegiate Dictionary* © 1977 by G. & C. Merriam Co., Publishers of the Merriam Webster Dictionaries, p. 750.

2. Adapted from the definition of the heart by the Puritan John Owen in his treatise *Indwelling Sin* (1656) as it appears in *Temptation and Sin* (reprint edition, Evansville, Ind.: Sovereign Grace Book Club, 1958), p. 7.

3. Owen, *Temptation and Sin*, p. 16. Author's paraphrase.

4. The Navigators' *Topical Memory System* may be obtained from www.NavPress.com.

5. Clarence H. Faust and Thomas H. Johnson, eds. *Jonathan Edwards — Representative Selections, with Introduction, Bibliography, and Notes* (revised edition, New York: Hill and Wang, 1962), p. 38.

Session Seven: **The Place of Personal Discipline**

1. Jay E. Adams, *Godliness Through Discipline* (P&R Press, 1999), p. 3.

2. Godliness is closely akin to holiness in Scripture. Strong's Concordance lists holiness as a synonym for godliness. Vine says godliness is "that piety which is characterized by a Godward attitude, and does that which is well pleasing to Him" (*Expository Dictionary of New Testament Words*, p. 162).

3. *Webster's New Collegiate Dictionary*, p. 325.

4. Adams, *Godliness Through Discipline*, p. 14.

5. The Navigators have materials to help you develop a Bible reading plan, start systematic Bible study, and begin a Scripture memory program. These materials are available from www.NavPress.com.

6. Clarence H. Faust and Thomas H. Johnson, eds. *Jonathan Edwards — Representative Selections, with Introduction, Bibliography, and Notes* (revised edition, New York: Hill and Wang, 1962), p. 43.

Session Eight: **Holiness in Body**

1. Michel Quoist, *The Christian Response* (Dublin: Gill and Macmillan, 1965), p. 4.

2. John Kirk, *The Mother of the Wesleys* (Cincinnati: Poe and Hitchcock, 1865), p. 178.

3. This quote from Thomas Boston is taken from an old magazine article in the author's files. Unfortunately, neither the title of the magazine nor the date of publication was listed on the clipping.

4. Adapted from the definition of the heart by the Puritan John Owen in his treatise *Indwelling Sin* (1656) as it appears in *Temptation and Sin* (reprint edition, Evansville, Ind.: Sovereign Grace Book Club, 1958), p. 31.

SESSION TEN: **Holiness and Our Wills**

1. In the *New International Version* the phrase from this verse reads, "Set your heart on things above." However, Paul evidently used *heart* here in its more limited meaning of affections or emotions, since in verse 2 he told us to set our minds — that is, our intellect — on things above. Thus he exhorted us to set both our affections and our reason on spiritual values.

2. The list of books which uniquely meet each person's needs will of course vary. My own list will not necessarily motivate the reader, but, for whatever it is worth, it includes *Romans: An Exposition of Chapter 6 — The New Man* by D. Martyn Lloyd-Jones, and *Temptation and Sin* by John Owen (both previously cited in this book); and two other short, readable books: *Power Through Prayer* by E. M. Bounds (Zondervan), and *The Life of Robert Murray McCheyne* by Andrew Bonar (Banner of Truth Trust). I must say, however, that day-in and day-out the Scriptures themselves motivate me more to holiness than all the books in my library.

3. John Owen, *Temptation and Sin* (Regent College: 1983), p. 253.

4. *Webster's New Collegiate Dictionary*, p. 514.

5. Owen, p. 28.

6. *Webster's New Collegiate Dictionary*, p. 514.

7. Owen, p. 40, author's paraphrase.

SESSION ELEVEN: **Holiness and Faith**

1. We have already observed in session 6 that sincere Christians disagree on what activities are appropriate for Sunday; nevertheless, this man was obeying God's will for him.

2. John Brown, *An Exposition of Hebrews* (1862; reprint edition, Edinburgh: The Banner of Truth Trust, 1961), p. 508.

SESSION TWELVE: **Holiness in an Unholy World**

1. From *New Testament Commentary: Exposition of the Gospel According to Matthew* by William Hendriksen (Grand Rapids, Mich.: Baker Book House, 1973), p. 282. Used by permission.

2. Charles G. Trumbull, *Taking Men Alive* (1907; reprint edition, Westwood, N. J.: Fleming H. Revell Co., 1938), p. 80.

3. From *New Testament Commentary: Exposition of the Gospel According to John* by William Hendriksen (Grand Rapids, Mich.: Baker Book House, 1953), p. 281. Used by permission.

About the Author

Jerry Bridges is an author and Bible teacher. His most popular book, *The Pursuit of Holiness*, has sold over one million copies. He is also the author of *Trusting God*, *The Discipline of Grace*, *The Fruitful Life*, *The Gospel for Real Life*, and *Respectable Sins*. As a full-time staff member with The Navigators for many years, Jerry has served in the collegiate ministry and community ministries.